ADVANCE

MW00412405

Shadows
Book #2 in THE SEVEN Trilogy
Fred Ellis Brock

Pub Date: January 2021

ISBN: 978-1-948018-92-0 Trade Paperback
212 pages, 5.5 x 8.5, $15.95

CATEGORIES:
FIC031000 Thrillers
FIC024000 Supernatural
FIC028000 Science Fiction
FIC028010 Science Fiction/Action & Adventure

DISTRIBUTED BY:
INGRAM, FOLLETT, COUTTS, MBS, YBP,
COMPLETE BOOK, BERTRAMS, GARDNERS
Or wholesale@wyattmackenzie.com

Wyatt-MacKenzie Publishing
DEADWOOD, OREGON

PUBLISHER CONTACT:
Nancy Cleary
nancy@wyattmackenzie.com

AGENT CONTACT:
David Black Literary Agency
Ayla Zuraw-Friedland, AZuraw-Friedland@dblackagency.com

AUTHOR CONTACT:
Fred Brock
feb2@mac.com

SHADOWS

SHADOWS

THE SECOND BOOK IN THE SEVEN TRILOGY
FRED ELLIS BROCK

Wyatt-MacKenzie Publishing
DEADWOOD, OREGON

SHADOWS
Fred Ellis Brock

The Second Novel in THE SEVEN Trilogy

ISBN: 978-1-948018-92-0 Trade Paperback
Library of Congress Control Number: 2020935679

Wyatt-MacKenzie Publishing
DEADWOOD, OREGON

Wyatt-MacKenzie Publishing, Inc., Deadwood, OR
www.wyattmackenzie.com

The Near Future

CHAPTER 1

Bill Sanders was distracted and not feeling well. He was jet-lagged and had a cold, which was not helped by the chilly and blustery March weather in New York. Nancy Luke, his literary agent, having recently returned from a two-week vacation in Barbados, looked tan and fit. Her hair was a bit longer and lighter than he remembered and didn't have the usual frosting or tiny bows. *That's an improvement; she looks more serious.* He mentally checked himself. *She's one of the top agents in New York. She's plenty serious. She stuck with me when I quit reporting and started writing books. She got me a million dollars from a Hollywood producer for the film rights to* Look Down. *Incredible for a first novel. The advance she just got for the Mideast book, based on a seven-page proposal, was more than I earned in five years as a top reporter.*

"The Manhattan clam chowder is excellent today," Gerald, their usual waiter at Dave's, commented as he took their drink orders. Bill ordered a neat Scotch; Nancy, a glass of Pinot Grigio. Bill and Nancy had been having lunches on the second Wednesday of the month at Dave's for years. It was midway between her office near Rockefeller Center and his Eastside Towers apartment on East Seventy-Second Street. It wasn't one of the best restaurants in New York, but Nancy liked it because it wasn't a literary hangout where people were always listening for gossip and tidbits of news.

"You look terrible, Bill. When did you get back?"

"Late yesterday afternoon. On a flight from Cairo that stopped in London. I caught a cold along the way. This Scotch will help."

"You need to take it easy. You've been traveling and working hard on the Mideast book since November and before that you went through that terrible situation in Indiana in the spring and summer. If I had known you were sick, I wouldn't have insisted on lunch today."

"I'm okay, really. I'm almost finished with the research. One more trip to Beirut and Cairo, and maybe Israel, and a few more days in D.C. should wind it up and then I can start writing."

"How long until you have a manuscript?"

"A year. Maybe eighteen months."

"Well, the contract with the publisher calls for a complete, publishable manuscript in eighteen months. However, with a three-month notice that deadline can be extended to two years. You may need that extra time. You just signed the contract, so any more travel or research eats into your writing time."

"I know. I know. Don't worry. I've never missed a deadline in my life. And I really do need to make this one more trip."

Gerald arrived with their drinks and took their orders. Both had a cup of the clam chowder. Bill ordered broiled salmon; Nancy had a Caesar salad with chicken, dressing on the side.

"Have you come up with a title yet? You always say you can't write a book until you have a title."

"It's not exactly that direct. But when I have a title, I also seem to have a better sense of how I'll write the book. I'm thinking of something along the lines of *Power Play* or *Power Points*, maybe with a subtitle. I guess the title's still a work in progress."

"Well, the reason I wanted to see you is that I have some interesting news."

"What's that?"

"You're going back to Indiana. Back to Jefferson."

"Whoa! I'm in the middle of a book. You were just bugging me about getting down to writing. There's no reason for me to go back there." *Actually, there're a lot of reasons for me not to go back there. Sharon blames me for Paul's death and hates my guts. I'd have a hard time looking Dave Taylor in the eye again without telling him that I stole evidence and then continued to withhold it in a murder case he regards as still unsolved. Do I tell him I know who killed Daniel Scott? Or that Paul's Jeep "accident" was murder? Or that Cindy was abducted, is dead, and I know where her ashes were dumped? Do I tell him I know who is behind this horror show and risk being portrayed as a drug-addled mental patient by The Seven? Dave wouldn't believe any of it anyway, especially if the letters UFO entered into the conversation. While probably a good sheriff, Dave is not particularly open minded on that subject, which I learned the hard way after I drove out to Jefferson last spring to help Paul. Plus, revisiting all this would lead me to dwell on Morgen, which is painful. But Nancy doesn't know any of this, although I promised to tell her everything about events in Jefferson. I know I'm being secretive again, but how can I tell a hard-nosed literary agent such an unbelievable story? She would probably think I was nuts. All she knows is that Cindy is stilling missing, Paul was killed in a car crash, and Daniel Scott was murdered in such a way as to make his death look like suicide. Which is about all anyone knows. Except me. And The Seven.*

"In fact, there is. Jack Turner called me the day before yesterday just after I learned he had been hired by English-Frostmann Studios to direct the movie version of *Look Down*. He wants to scout Jefferson as a possible location for filming. And he wants to hire you as a consultant.

"But why Jefferson? Why me?"

"Well, *Look Down* is your somewhat autobiographical novel that mostly takes place in a small Midwest town like the one you grew up in. You're the expert. Makes perfect sense to me. It's not a done deal, but I think Jack really wants to film on location in Jefferson. He's a top director. I've known him for years. We can't say no to him. He wants you to meet him in Jefferson as soon as possible so you can show him around and help check out locations for various scenes. I think you two will get along famously. You've seen Chris Wade's screenplay, which you liked. It shouldn't take more than a week. That couldn't throw too much of a monkey wrench into your schedule or plans. Imagine what an economic boon it would be for a small town to have a major movie studio encamped for weeks, spending all that money."

You weren't enthusiastic about me going out there last year to help Paul. But now there's a business reason for it, so I guess I see the logic to your change of mind. "Well, I have some reservations. I know Jack Turner's a big Hollywood name—I watch the Academy Awards—but I don't really know anything about him. But you know I trust your judgment. When do I leave?"

"I'll call Jack and let you know. The studio will of course pay all your expenses, plus a nice consulting fee which I'm still negotiating upward. And you'll like this: Jack said he would send the English-Frostmann corporate jet to fly you from Teterboro to Jefferson. And back.

A really powerful and important organization—it seemed to be The National Geographic Society—had hired Bill to investigate an airliner crash near JFK airport in New York. Morgen Remley was working with him in the investigation. First, he talked to some reporter friends who were covering it for Newsday on Long Island. He then read about the crash in The New York Times, which also printed a number of pictures. From the pictures, it seemed the plane had crashed into some kind of field with rows of crops, and the crash site was in the middle of three big towers that carry electric lines. The plane could only have crashed in one direction so as not to have hit these towers and lines. He wasn't sure what more he could learn about the crash, but he and Morgen decided to go ahead anyway.

For some reason they were in Brooklyn and had to arrange for transportation to the crash site. Bill called a taxi, but it failed to show up. They walked around for a while trying to hail another taxi, but all were either occupied or off duty. Morgen tried to call Uber, but her cell phone wouldn't work; Bill couldn't find his phone, although he was certain he had put it into his pocket earlier. Then they walked around a corner and noticed a storefront with a sign reading "Car Service. Expert Drivers." They opened the front door and stepped into a large, smoke-filled room with weird, bizarre-looking people sitting in wooden chairs up against the walls. They were drivers waiting for assignments.

Bill found the manager in a dirty little alcove in the back of the room. He agreed to rent them a car and driver for the trip to the crash site. They picked a driver who looked the best of the lot, which Bill thought wasn't saying much. Morgen seemed nervous. Bill told the manager they needed the car and driver for three or four hours; the manager said the price would be one thousand dollars. Bill exploded in anger, yelling that the price was too high, that he and Morgen were on an important mission for The National Geographic Society. The manager agreed to lower the price to five hundred dollars.

The driver they had selected seemed to know all about the crash site and how to get to it. But first the three had to pass through a kind of no-man's land near the airport. The area was sinister and littered with aircraft pieces that had fallen off planes over the years as they had landed or taken off. Bill thought the public would be upset if this were known.

Then they were at the field and near the crash site. It looked just like the pictures in the Times. As Bill and Morgen were walking to the site past the crop rows, the driver told them they were not allowed to see what was going on along the third row, where men in white coats were doing something. They acted very secretive and covered up what they were working on with green sheets as Bill and Morgen passed by. At the site itself, rescue workers were putting bodies on stretchers. Bill looked at one victim who the workers said was dead. It was Jane! As he looked in horror at the face of his dead wife, she opened and closed her eyes. For a brief moment she looked right at Bill.

Bill grabbled the workers by their white coats. "She's alive, you fucking idiots!" he screamed. "She's not dead!" The workers insisted he was wrong and went on with their work. Bill discovered he had a camera, which he didn't remember bringing. He set it on a very high shutter speed in an attempt to get a picture of Jane with her eyes open.

Suddenly, the camera started to ring....

Bill fumbled for the camera but then came fully awake and realized he was holding the receiver of his bedside phone.

"Hello."

"Bill, it's Nancy. Did I wake you up?"

Bill glanced at his watch. Nine-thirty. Friday.

"Yeah. I'm still nursing that cold, but it's better. Can I call you back in a half hour or so when I'm more awake?"

"Sure. I'm in the office."

"Okay. Later."

Bill, shaken by the intensity of his dream, lay back on the bed. After Jane, Bill's wife of twenty-six years, was killed a little more than three years ago when the plane she was flying from Paris to New York was destroyed by a terrorist's bomb over Newfoundland, he started having a recurring dream of him trying but failing to stop her from boarding the flight. That dream had started fading after events in Jefferson last year and his subsequent involvement with Morgen. But other dreams had moved into his head. Strange dreams that he was trying to understand, like the one he just had in which Jane appeared to be alive. What the hell was that supposed to mean? What was going on in the third row that he and Morgen weren't allowed to see? Morgen often appeared in these latest dreams, but this was the first in which she and Jane both were present. Bill had read enough psychology and Carl Jung and Joseph Campbell to know that dreams speak in symbols and metaphors not easily understood by the conscious mind. After Jane's death, he dismissed the idea of seeing a psychiatrist. He was simply too private, or, as Jane used to say, secretive. Maybe he would change his mind, but not now. Probably never. He was what he was. He *was* often secretive and didn't like being the center of attention. His brown hair and average looks and height allowed him to blend into almost any situation. People he interviewed never felt threatened by him. He knew he wasn't the story. They were. His fellow reporters regarded him as a master of getting interview subjects, especially politicians, to say things they often regretted later. People liked talking to Bill because he was a good listener. He seldom interrupted and was adept at using silence as a tool to get people to talk. Learn to shut up and listen, he advised young reporters. Those features and skills served him well when he and Jane spent two years traveling around Mexico and Central and South America researching *Points South*, his breakthrough book.

His mind shifted from Jane to Morgen, the woman he had come to love and who had betrayed him. Thinking of her always brought a mixture of anger, sadness, and longing. He knew he should hate her, but he couldn't. He loved her. He missed her. He wanted to be with her. He wondered how she, wherever she was, felt about him. Despite the warning from Colonel West, Bill had gone to her apartment in Brooklyn a few days after he was returned, alone and hooded, to East Seventy-Second Street. Morgen's apartment was vacant and being renovated and repainted. The workmen knew nothing of any former tenants. What about Brenda Jones, Morgen's roommate from Kansas? Was she just an actor hired by The Seven to help set Bill up? Remembering Colonel West's warning, Bill returned to Manhattan and never again asked questions or looked for Morgen. Even when Colonel West died, Bill knew the file he had been shown was still in the hands of The Seven.

As he had done many times during the past year, Bill replayed in his mind fragmented images of the events that led him to Indiana and Morgen and The Seven. And now he was returning to a place where only he and some ultra-top-secret government operatives know its shadows and secrets. He would never forget the fear and panic in Paul Watson's voice last spring when his best friend since the fifth grade called from their hometown of Jefferson, Indiana. *I'm afraid. You're the only person who can help me.* Paul refused to disclose any details, imploring Bill to come to Jefferson as soon as possible. Having finished *Look Down* and unsure about his next book project, Bill agreed. When he arrived in Jefferson, Bill discovered that Paul's ten-year-old daughter, Cindy, had gone missing two weeks earlier, and his wife had left him. The police thought the girl was a runaway, but Paul, who had started drinking heavily, confided to Bill that he had witnessed her being abducted by a UFO. Paul told this to only two other people: Sharon, his wife, and Dave Taylor, the county Sheriff.

Sharon became hysterical and left Paul, embarrassed by his account; Dave thought he was a mental case, but, because they were friends, kept the story out of any official reports and never mentioned it to anyone until he discussed it with Bill last year.

Tears blurred Bill's vision as he remembered Paul. Poor Paul. Dead. Murdered in a horrific way. Along with his daughter, Cindy, and Daniel Scott, a promising young reporter for The Jefferson Courier. *And I know the truth but cannot tell it.*

✳

Bill showered and shaved before returning Nancy Luke's call.

"Nancy, I'm sorry for the delay. I had been sound asleep and needed a few minutes to get my stuffy head together."

"No problem. I just wanted to tell you that I talked to Jack Turner late last night. I didn't call you then because I knew you weren't feeling great and were probably asleep. He wants you to fly out to Jefferson Monday morning at eight. That's when the plane is scheduled to meet you at Teterboro. I gather it's less than a two-hour flight. He assured me that the pilot assured him that the general aviation airport's runway at Jefferson is long enough to accommodate a small corporate jet. He said a rental car would be waiting for you, and you have reservations at the Jefferson Hotel. Wasn't that where you stayed for a while last year after your friend was killed?"

"Yes. You have a good memory."

"Well, there's the Jefferson Hotel in Washington where I usually stay when I'm down there. I guess my memory picked up on that. Anyway, Jack will arrive Monday evening. Apparently, after dropping you off, the plane will fly from Jefferson to Los Angeles, pick him up and then fly back to Jefferson. They clearly have plenty of money in Hollywood. An assistant will be with him. A woman by the name of Joan Wilson. I don't know anything about her. Jack said he would call your cell when they got to the airport. He also promised me this would only tie you up for a week or so. It's the 'or so' part that worries me. By the way, Jack didn't hesitate an iota when I strongly suggested he double his initial offer for your consulting fee."

"You're amazing."

"I'm glad you noticed. Hurry back. You've got a lot of writing to do."

Bill spent the rest of the day going through and organizing his notes and files for the Mideast book. When he got back from Jefferson, he would start planning his last research trip to the region. After that, he would spend a week or so in D.C. for some final interviews.

Despite nursing the remnants of a cold, Bill decide to walk around the corner and have dinner at an Italian restaurant he liked. He was putting his windbreaker jacket on when the phone rang.

"Hello."

"Bill? Bill Sanders?"

"Yes."

"Bill, it's Graham Neal."

"Neal! What a pleasure. How the hell are you?"

He had never been called anything but Neal.

"Okay, I guess. But almost a year older and sadder since we last talked. I'm really not over the murder of Daniel Scott. The Sheriff and State Police still don't have suspect one, despite considerable pressure from the paper. Nothing new on Cindy Watson's disappearance either." *Oh God, Neal, if only I could tell you the truth.*

"Thanks for letting me know, even if there's nothing new. I've been mostly out of the country for the past few months working on a new book about the Mideast."

"I saw something about that on the AP wire a month or so back. But the real reason I called is I'm trying to chase down a rumor that a major movie studio is thinking of filming *Look Down* in Jefferson. I figured if anybody would know, it would be you."

"It's true. Maybe it's supposed to be confidential, but nobody told me. In fact, I'm flying out there Monday to meet Jack Turner, the director English-Frostmann Studios hired. He wants to look at possible locations in Jefferson."

"Sweet Jesus! Jack Turner. Mr. Hollywood. That's amazing. Do you have any idea what a project like that would mean to Jefferson?"

"Neal, it's not a done deal. He's coming for a scouting expedition. But I will tell you that I think he really wants Jefferson. The studio is flying me out there on its corporate jet, so they must be serious. I wish you would hold off on running anything until I get there on Monday, but I know you won't. I wouldn't either If I were in your place. I really don't know anything else except that I'll be arriving at Jefferson Field sometime before noon; Turner will be flying in later that day. I'm not sure exactly when. He's bringing an assistant with him named Joan Wilson. We'll all be at the Jefferson Hotel for about a week. I don't know him or her, but I'll do everything I can to get him to cooperate with you. Of course, if Turner settles on Jefferson, you're going to have the Louisville, Indianapolis, and Cincinnati papers and TV and radio breathing down your neck, not to mention the national media. It'll be a circus. But I'll try my best to make sure you get first shot at anything interesting or exclusive. Fair enough?"

"Oh, hell yes. I knew hiring you back then would pay off someday. Speaking of hiring, I hired Daniel Scott's cousin to fill that reporting slot. He came to me and wanted the job. I couldn't say no. His name is John King. He was an English major at the University of Chicago but turned out to be a quick study in news reporting. He's solid. He was never into African-American politics like Daniel, who saw journalism as a way to change things. John's a little more laid back. You'll meet him. I'm assigning him to this story."

"Okay. I'll see you Monday then."

"Yep. And this time I hope you can make it to dinner. Marge would be delighted to see you. I still know how to make a martini."

"Count on it. Oh, one more thing. Where is Sharon Watson? Still in Indianapolis?"

"Yes. She moved there after Paul's death to be near her parents. I don't think she could stand being in Jefferson and constantly reminded of Cindy. Oddly, she never sold their house. It's been sitting there, locked up, for almost a year. A neighbor apparently checks on it once a month. I wonder if she's keeping the house in the hope that Cindy will return someday and have a familiar place to return to?"

"Maybe. That is a bit strange. Well, see you Monday. Probably early in the afternoon."

"Okay. Bye."

Bill was very fond of Neal. He was the editor of the Jefferson Courier, a paper Neal's family had owned for almost a century. He had hired Bill to cover basketball games while he was in high school and later hired him as a reporter during the summers between his college years. After Bill graduated, he moved on to bigger newspapers: The Louisville Courier-Journal, The Houston Chronicle, and, finally, The New York Times, where he worked in the paper's Washington bureau. Although he left journalism more than a decade ago to write books, he never forgot Neal and what he learned from him about writing and human nature in general.

I wish I could level with him. Maybe someday.

CHAPTER 2

The ranch house room was not big; it seemed even smaller because of the large conference table in its center. Three men in business suits sat on one side. On the other side were two women and a man dressed more casually than the first three. Another, older man, also dressed in casual clothes, sat at the head of the table. At the other end was an empty chair.

Outside, a worker was painting the front porch. Nearby a barn and corral looked perfectly normal. The only things that might give a visitor pause were the painter's Glock pistol in a leather holster hanging from his right side and a helipad and windsock behind the barn, not far from an unmarked satellite dish that was far too big and sophisticated for commercial television.

The ranch house and surrounding structures were in the center of a ten-thousand-acre ranch in southern New Mexico, near the border with Mexico. All roads on the property had been bulldozed over and blocked with iron barriers. The only way in and out was by helicopter, all-terrain vehicle, or foot. No matter how visitors arrived, their presence would be picked up and they would be tracked by sophisticated electronic devices hidden in the ground, in trees, and in fence posts.

The original ranch house had been torn down and replaced by one that, from the outside, looked much the same. Inside the house, however, were offices and an elevator leading to underground rooms crammed with computers and communications equipment, as well as other offices and living quarters. It was one of two such facilities in the United States.

The other was in Ulster County, in upstate New York not far from the small town of Pine Bush.

The man at the head of the table was speaking.

"Where do we stand on Snakebite?"

"We need a little more time, maybe a month or two, to get all the elements in place," one of the suits replied. "The coordination has to be precise."

"Take the time you need. We only have one shot at this, and we have to get it right. We don't want to take forever, but there's no pressing deadline."

Everyone at the table nodded in agreement.

"What about the reductions we talked about? The numbers of people reporting to us have become so large that I think they risk our security and ability to remain secret. People like Colonel West had too many people working for him. Some of them got out of control. That's how we got into trouble in Indiana. We're very tightly compartmentalized, but the more people we allow in the tent the more porous we become. The more mistakes we make."

One of the women spoke up.

"That's my department. We're starting to tighten down. We have carefully created incriminating evidence on a certain percentage of the people who work for us and are expendable. Some of it is fake, like the file West showed that writer—his name is Bill Sanders—in Pine Bush. Some of it is real. Our agents are very good. If that doesn't keep them quiet, there's always Plan B."

"Which we should try to avoid. That way can get very messy, as we saw in Indiana."

"Yes, of course. Only as a last resort."

"Any other problems I need to know about?"

"I don't think so," replied the second suit. "Colonel West's plan to silence that writer if he didn't agree to join us appears to be working. Not a peep out of him. He's busy with another book, and a big Hollywood studio is making a movie out of his novel."

"Good. But keep an occasional eye on him. We can always

revert to our original plan, but only if we have no other choice. Holden's no longer a threat to us, but what he left behind might be. One of our people thinks he had lists of some of our members that could be damaging. Those two file cabinets we got right after he died last year contained no lists or anything of value to us. But we have to start looking again, even more aggressively."

The other woman at the table looked up from some notes she was taking.

"'Could be' is an understatement. We have to find those lists at all cost. Especially if he had any documents or information linking the lists to us. He must have had something else. Just lists of names by themselves don't prove anything."

"Agreed. Let's double down on that. Maybe he hid the lists and other information somewhere else in his house. Also, let's keep an eye on the woman who brought Bill Sanders to us. What's her name?"

"Morgen."

"Right. Morgen Remley. I think she's solid, but let's be sure."

CHAPTER 3

The English-Frostmann plane banked over the Ohio River as it began its final descent into Jefferson Field. Bill, who had been dozing for most of the flight west, had a panoramic view of the town nestled among the Southern Indiana hills, tight against the river. He could see the copper dome of the Madison County courthouse glinting in the sun, which was peeking through increasingly dark clouds.

The sight of the courthouse led him to think of Sheriff Dave Taylor—and to flush with guilt. He and the Sheriff had made an agreement last year to share any and all information about Cindy Watson's disappearance and subsequent events in Jefferson. The Sheriff kept his part of the bargain; Bill didn't. In fact, he stole and concealed a map that may have been evidence in a murder case. He also didn't tell Dave Taylor about the threatening note he received the night Paul's house was ransacked. He had wanted to come clean with the Sheriff, but now was unsure after his meeting with the late Colonel Richard West. In an inside pocket of his backpack, next to his laptop, Bill had stashed three things just before leaving earlier in the morning for Teterboro: the map he had taken from Daniel Scott's room in a residence hotel after the reporter was killed; the warning note he found in his duffel bag following the break-in at Paul's; and Paul's house key, which he had forgotten to return to Sharon when he fled Jefferson for New York in a panic last year. Daniel had been covering Cindy's disappearance, but knew nothing of Paul's claim that she was abducted by a UFO. But there had been earlier UFO sightings around Jefferson, which Daniel covered for the Courier. The map of the county that Bill took was covered with a random series of Xs and Os. At the bottom, in Daniel's handwriting, were two notations: "O = UFO sightings" and "X = helicopters." It was the reference to helicopters that caused Bill to take the map.

✳

As Bill lifted his duffel and backpack down the plane's stairs to the tarmac, a stranger walked up and took his picture several times with an expensive Nikon.

The stranger stuck out his hand.

"Hi, Mr. Sanders. I'm Jeff Keefer, the photographer for the Jefferson Courier. Welcome to Jefferson."

"Call me Bill. Neal sent you?"

"Yep. Do you mind climbing back on the plane's stairs for a couple more shots?"

"Sure. No problem."

The photographer took a few more photos of Bill walking down the stairs.

"Thanks. I've got to run. Another assignment."

"If you talk to Neal, tell him I'll see him this afternoon."

"Will do. Thanks again."

Bill was walking into a gated area when the pilot retracted the stairs and started the engines. He and the co-pilot waved and began to taxi out to the single runway. Bill put his duffel down and waved back. They were headed to California to pick up Jack Turner and Joan Wilson.

As promised, a rental car was waiting for him. A full-size Buick. Bill presented his New York driver's license and an American Express card to an obviously bored clerk in the airport's cramped and dingy office, signed and initialed some papers, and was on his way to the Jefferson Hotel. The airport was only about a fifteen-minute drive from the center of town. But that can be a long time when the past takes over. This was Bill's second trip to Jefferson in less than a year. Before then, he had only been to Jefferson three times since graduating from Indiana University almost thirty years ago. Twice for the funerals of his mother and father and once for the funeral of his younger brother, who was killed in a prison fight in Texas, where he was serving a life sentence for killing a deputy sheriff in a drunken brawl. Bill had never attended a high school class reunion; the only person from Jefferson he kept in touch with was Paul Watson.

He vividly remembered his reaction to Paul's UFO story: anger and disbelief. But he agreed to hear Paul out and, in the end, although convinced Paul was delusional, agreed to help search for his missing daughter. Bill also discovered there had been a number of UFO sightings around Jefferson during the past year; one security guard he and Paul talked to recalled seeing strange lights accompanied by the sound of helicopters. Bill began to believe Paul may have seen something unexplainable. But Bill was very circumspect in talking with the Sheriff and Graham Neal, both of whom ridiculed any references to UFOs. Dave Taylor told Bill that Paul needed psychiatric help.

Events took a sinister turn when Paul's house was ransacked and Bill received an anonymous message warning him to forget his friend and return to New York; "Remember Jane," the second sentence of the warning said. Next, Daniel Scott, the local reporter who had been investigating Cindy's disappearance, was found shot dead with a gun in his hand. His death was ruled a suicide until Bill convinced the Sheriff to run a paraffin test, which proved the reporter did not fire the gun. He was murdered. It was then that Bill slipped unnoticed into Daniel's room at a residence hotel, discovered the map, and took it.

Two days later Paul was killed in a mysterious auto crash that the police ruled accidental, even though moments before the crash a farmer saw a low-flying, black helicopter over Paul's speeding Jeep. Paul had been drinking, a fact that Dave Taylor kept under wraps.

Bill was stumped, unsure where to turn or what to do. He was convinced that events in Jefferson were over the head of the local Sheriff. Finally, he called an old friend, a former United States senator from New Mexico named Warren Holden, who had longtime ties to the U.S. intelligence community and once held Senate hearings on UFO sightings. Holden, whose main area of interest was South America, had been a major source for *Points South*; he had a secondary interest in the Middle East.

*

Bill's mind refocused on the present when he saw the Jefferson Hotel just ahead on his left. He pulled into the parking lot, surrounded by leafless trees that had been green and welcoming last summer but now looked vaguely threatening, their bare boney branches pointing toward an increasingly leaden sky. There were traces of dirty snow on the edges of the parking lot. He sat in the car for a few minutes, with the engine running, trying to clear his mind of Paul and Cindy Watson and Daniel Scott.

Bill carried his duffel and backpack into the lobby. The desk clerk seemed surprised to see him.

"I have a reservation. Bill Sanders."

"Oh yes, Mr. Sanders. We weren't expecting you this early."

"I know I'm a bit early. Is it okay if I check in now?"

"Sure. This isn't a busy time for us. Your room is ready. Room thirty-seven on the third floor. Elevators are behind the front desk. I'm sorry you had to carry your bags in. Our bellman called in sick today. But I can take them to your room for you."

"No, that's fine. I can manage."

"Are you sure?"

"I'm sure. Do you have a copy of Saturday's Courier?" The local afternoon paper didn't have a Sunday edition, and Bill knew the Monday paper wouldn't be available until later in the afternoon.

The clerk pointed to a stack of papers to Bill's right.

"Help yourself. No charge."

On the front page was a big banner headline:

HOLLYWOOD COMING TO JEFFERSON?

Under it were two-column pictures of Jack Turner and Bill. The story had John King's and Neal Graham's double by-line on it. Bill was cited as the only source for the story; it was mostly interviews with local businessmen about how great it would be for Jefferson to have a major movie made in their town.

The desk clerk suddenly realized the Bill Sanders who had just registered was the Bill Sanders on page one.

"Oh, Mr. Sanders. I didn't recognize you. What an honor to have you here again. I remember you were here last summer. We don't get many famous people around here. I just finished *Look Down*. Loved it. Can't wait for the movie. Mr. Turner and Ms. Wilson will be checking in later today."

"I know. Thanks."

"If you need anything, just call the front desk. I'm Steve. By the way, there's a full buffet breakfast in the lobby from six to ten."

✳

Bill liked the room. There was a big bed, a small sofa, a wingback chair, a coffee table, and a small desk and chair. After unpacking his duffel, Bill lay on the bed, pillows propping up his head, and read the rest of the Saturday Courier. He looked at the real estate ads, amazed at how inexpensive property and homes were in Jefferson. *I've been living in New York too long.*

Suddenly realizing he was hungry, Bill washed his face, combed his hair and glanced out the window. The sky had grown more overcast and the wind had picked up. The bare tree branches around the parking lot were gently bending to the south.

Bill dialed the front desk.

"Steve, this is Bill Sanders. What's the temperature outside?"

"Right now, it's forty-two. But it's supposed to go down to below freezing tonight. Wind's picking up so it feels colder."

"Okay, thanks." Bill suddenly realized he could have gotten this information from his cell phone, but he also realized he enjoyed talking to people and was more than a little hesitant about modern technology anyway. His work forced him to master computer skills, but he hated reading on a computer screen. He also didn't like GPS devices. He liked books and papers and maps.

Bill pulled a wool sweater over his shirt for extra warmth under his windbreaker. He wanted to get some lunch and then visit Neal at the Courier office. He discovered last year that Neal still always went home from noon until one to have lunch with Marge. The two had been inseparable since they were sweethearts in high school.

Despite the chill and the wind, Bill decided to walk six blocks to the Jefferson Cafe, just across Main Street from the courthouse where he and Dave Taylor had first talked last year. It used to be the Douglas Sandwich Shop when Bill was a student at Jefferson High. When Mrs. Douglas died, the new owners remodeled and renamed it. The food was still good.

Bill smiled as his walk took him past Hink's Hamburger Heaven, a twenty-four-hour joint that had been a fixture in Jefferson for decades and still looked pretty much the same as when he was eighteen years old. The smell of greasy hamburgers permeated Hink's side of the street. When he first arrived in Jefferson last spring, Bill had a couple of the burgers for old-time's sake.

It was pleasantly warm in the Jefferson Cafe; Bill settled into an empty booth and studied a menu.

"Bill Sanders, you son of a gun!"

Bill looked up to see Sheriff Dave Taylor standing next to him. Bill stood up and they shook hands.

"Mind if I join you?"

"Please do. We can catch up." Both settled into the booth.

"I read in the paper that you were coming to town. On a private jet, yet. Are they really going to make that movie here?

And Jack Turner's coming to town?"

"Yep, later today. I understand he's just considering Jefferson but hasn't made up his mind yet. But my agent thinks he really wants to shoot the film here. She knows him and has talked to him. I don't know him at all. He's bringing an assistant I don't know either. I'm pretty much in the dark like everyone else. Guess we'll know one way or the other soon."

"Well, a major studio like English-Frostmann making a film here would sure set this town hoppin' high."

"I bet."

A server with the name Becky embroidered on her uniform interrupted to take their orders. Both ordered coffee and the day's special, pot roast and mashed potatoes with a salad.

"So how have you been? Guess rushing back to New York last year when you had that book crisis paid off. *Look Down* has been at the top of every best-seller list since. Every time I turn around, I see an article about you or the novel."

I rushed back to New York because I thought someone was trying to kill me. Turns out I was right. At least until Colonel West intervened. I'm caught in a pack of lies I can't back out of without destroying myself. I wonder how many copies of that file The Seven has.

"I had no idea it would do this well when I was writing it."

"You're working on another book now?"

"Yes. It's kind of a Mideast version of *Points South*, the nonfiction book I did on Mexico and Central and South America. I've been working on it since last November. Just research. Haven't written anything yet, but plan to start soon."

"You haven't missed much around here. It's been pretty quiet since that craziness last spring with Cindy Watson vanishing and then Paul dying in a car crash and Daniel Scott getting murdered. Thanks to you we know Daniel was killed and didn't commit suicide."

"Reporter's sixth sense, I guess. Anything new on Cindy or Daniel?" *Here I go. Getting in deeper. Asking questions that I already know the answers to.*

"Not a damn thing. The State Police and the FBI are still

officially on the cases, but between you and me I think they've pretty much thrown up their hands. Neal's been pushing me pretty hard, especially about Daniel. But I don't know what else to do. No clues. No suspects. No nothing. We were able to trace the thirty-eight special that killed Daniel to its last owner, an old lady who lived in Las Vegas and died eleven years ago. She reported the gun stolen two years before she died. One of the state troopers assigned to the case got a bug up her butt that Paul was involved in his daughter's disappearance. I went back over the details of the case and set her straight. Remember, Paul was drinking with friends and Sharon was asleep."

"I understand she's still in Indianapolis."

"She is. To my knowledge, she hasn't been back since Paul's funeral. She kept their house here. It's locked up, and I think a neighbor looks in on it. I heard she pays that same neighbor's kid to mow the grass once a week. Our night deputy usually makes a point of driving by to check on it at least two or three times a week. Last fall he found some kids camping in the yard, but they weren't hurting anything. I think Sharon had some kind of a nervous breakdown after Cindy's disappearance and Paul's death. That's a lot to deal with. On top of that, she had to cope with that loopy UFO abduction story Paul told her and you and me. I guess we're still the only three people who know about that."

"I guess." *Except for a secret government organization of God-knows-how-many killers.*

"Remember our agreement to share information?" the Sheriff asked.

"Of course, I do."

"Can we stick to that agreement, at least until these cases are solved or closed?"

"Absolutely."

"Is there anything you can tell me?"

"Not really ... maybe. Not long after the last time we talked on the phone, when I was beginning to get ready to go to the Middle East for an extended time, I called Sharon. She had found out from some notes in Paul's desk that I knew about his UFO story. She was angry because I didn't call her the minute Paul told me. She thought the UFO story was evidence he was having a psychotic breakdown and that may have been a factor in his Jeep crash. I tried to explain that she had already left for Indianapolis by the time Paul told me, and I had come to believe he saw something he couldn't explain. Maybe a helicopter. She cursed me, screamed that we might have saved him, and said she never wanted to talk to me or see me again. She hung up before I could point out that she could have acted without me. As I understand it, Paul told you about the UFO after he told Sharon. Did you know he had told her?"

"Yes, but I never discussed it with her. I was going to at some point, but she left town. I could have called her but didn't. You know what I thought about Paul's UFO story. I believe he was hallucinating. He had been drinking heavily for some time. I thought he needed psychiatric help. Sounds like Sharon was trying to lay some guilt on you. Why didn't you tell me about this?"

"I was really busy and didn't think it was important. Personal, I thought. I believed she was understandably irrational and was blindly striking out."

"You're probably right. So, you think Paul may have seen a helicopter? I guess that explains the questions you kept asking about helicopters. I know I was a little touchy on the subject. But I was fed up with all those crazy UFO sightings by drunks and kids on pot."

"I understand your frustration." *Except for the helicopters the night watchman heard whenever he saw those strange shafts of light at night. And the black helicopter that I later learned from Colonel West forced Paul to crash his Jeep into a culvert.*

Becky returned with their coffee and salads. The cafe was filling up with the lunch crowd; only a few seats were left. They were only halfway through their salads when Becky showed up again with two steaming plates of pot roast, mashed potatoes and succotash. Bill smiled to himself. He hadn't tasted succotash since he was in college. Maybe he would suggest they start serving it at Dave's. He wondered if

Nancy Luke—she was from a rich family and grew up in New York, Martha's Vineyard, and Europe—had ever tasted succotash.

When the two had finished lunch, Bill insisted on picking up the check.

"Well, thank you. They give me free coffee here in the morning, but that's the only freebee I take. Worries me that Neal might find out about that."

"I remember last year they wouldn't let me pay for my coffee or pie either because I was with you. My lips are sealed. Anyway, thank English-Frostmann for lunch. They're paying my expenses for this trip."

The two promised to stay in touch.

"Your cell number still the same? I remember your phone got smashed up in that break-in at Paul's last year."

"I got a new phone, but the number's the same."

"You can always reach me through my office number, or at home. That break-in was another mystery we never solved. Strange."

Not if you know the whole story.

With a wave, the Sheriff headed across Main Street to his office. Bill zipped up his windbreaker and headed to the Courier office a few blocks away.

Sarah Wong jumped up from her desk when Bill walked into the Courier's newsroom. She gave him a hug.

"Welcome back, stranger. I've been expecting you. When did you get in town?"

"This morning. A little before eleven."

"You're staying at the Jefferson Hotel, right?"

"Yes, for at least a week."

Sarah was in her early sixties and was one of the few people who had been at the paper when Bill worked there during his college summers. She was a Chinese American whose family had lived in Jefferson for well over a century. Her ancestors came to the American Midwest in the 1860s to work on the railroads; some of them liked Jefferson and stayed on. By the 1920s, the Wongs owned a successful hardware store that was still going strong. Sarah's family all worked there; she had an independent streak and staked out her own career at the newspaper office, where she had been the office manager for years. She knew everything about the Courier and kept it running smoothly. Neal often called her his most valuable employee.

"Is Neal back from lunch yet?"

"Any minute now. In fact, here he comes."

Neal walked through the paper's big front door, and his face beamed when he saw Bill. He quickened his pace and gave Bill a bear hug.

"Damn, it's good to see you again. You got away so fast last year that I never got to really say goodbye or even have you over for dinner. I'll be in serious trouble with Marge if that happens again."

"Don't worry. I'm here for at least a week. Just name a night."

"Let me talk to Marge."

Neal motioned for Bill to follow him down a hallway to his office, closing the door after they were in.

Neal reclined in his leather desk chair, propping his feet on his big wooden desk. Bill took a seat in an overstuffed chair in front of the desk.

"So, have you seen Saturday's paper?"

"Got one at the hotel as soon as I checked in."

"It was pretty thin, but it was all we had. Thanks to you. But hell, we got the jump on everybody else. This afternoon's story is also weak. Mainly man-on-the-street interviews with locals about what they think of the possibility of a major studio making a movie here. It's funny. A lot of people know who you are and that you're from here, but hardly anyone actually knows you. You've been away too long."

"Well, I've been a little busy since I graduated from IU and left Jefferson."

"Yeah, I know. But let's cut to the chase. Jack Turner's arriving later today, right?"

"Yes. He's coming from California. I'm not sure what time he'll arrive, but he'll call my cell when he does. I think I mentioned when you called me Friday that we're both staying at the Jefferson Hotel, along with his assistant. A woman named Joan Wilson."

"You did. But what I want you to do is introduce me and John King to Jack Turner and tell him we're good guys he should trust. In fact, I'd like to have the whole bunch—you, Jack Turner, Joan Wilson, and John—to my house for dinner."

Suddenly, Neal picked up his desk phone and punched a speed-dial number.

"Marge, honey, could you handle a dinner party tomorrow night at seven? Counting you and me, there'll be six people. One of them will be Jack Turner, the Hollywood director. Bill Sanders will be there, too. And John King. And a woman named Joan Wilson, who is Jack Turner's assistant."

Bill couldn't hear Marge's response, but Neal smiled at Bill.

"That's great. All the guests don't know about it yet, but what else are they going to do tomorrow night in a small town? If we have to change it, I'll let you know as soon as I can. Get Louise to come in for some extra hours to help out. Okay, great. Talk to you later. I love you."

Neal gently hung up the phone.

"Louise is our housekeeper. Been with us for fifteen or sixteen years. I'll leave Jack Turner and Joan Wilson a message at the hotel inviting them for dinner tomorrow. I'm assuming dinner then is okay with you. Marge is dying to see you again."

"Sure."

Bill looked at Neal across the big desk and smiled.

"You're still the Neal I remember from a long time ago. You're hustling me, just like I would do if I were in your place. Watching somebody like you work, it's no wonder I turned into a pretty good reporter."

"Better than pretty good, Bill. A lot better than pretty good."

They were interrupted by a knock on the door. Sarah Wong opened the door and came into Neal's office.

"Sorry to interrupt. Neal, you need to sign these two forms from the bank."

Neal glanced at the forms, signed them, and handed them back to Sarah. She nodded and left the office.

"I had lunch with Dave Taylor today. Ran into him at the Jefferson Cafe. He said you had been pushing him pretty hard on the Daniel Scott case."

"I guess. But, damn, you'd think he could come up with something after almost a year. Daniel's parents are very sweet and patient, but they deserve closure."

They may never get it. Neither will Sharon. At least Mr. and Mrs. Scott know Daniel is dead; Sharon will likely go to her grave never knowing what happened to Cindy.

"Maybe you ought to ease up on him a bit. I've stayed loosely in touch with him, and I know he and the State Police are doing all they can to solve Daniel's murder, as well as Cindy's disappearance. They are just very tough cases. Even the FBI is stumped about Cindy."

"You're probably right."

On the way back to the hotel, Bill happened to walk by the Oasis, a bar that had been on Main Street in Jefferson for as far back as he could remember. He decided to drop in and have a beer. It was a little after two. He guessed the plane from California wouldn't arrive until at least six or later.

Despite some remodeling, the bar looked pretty much the same as it did more than three decades ago, when the owner, Ralph Singer, used to serve beer to an underage Bill Sanders because he was usually with a group of reporters and editors from the Courier. Singer was an old man then. He must be dead now, Bill thought.

There was no one else in the bar. Not even a bartender was visible. Bill took a seat on a padded stool in front of a long wooden bar with decades of scratches and white rings from drink glasses and beer mugs. He faced a huge mirror that made the long narrow room seem bigger. Behind him were a row of narrow booths and two tables that looked new. Bill couldn't remember the bar having any booths or tables.

The bartender, who had been squatting behind the bar adjusting some glasses on a shelf, suddenly rose in front of Bill. He was short and stout with graying red hair. He gave Bill a puzzled look.

"What can I get for you?"

"What do you have on draft?"

"Bud. Bud Lite. Miller High Life. And Heineken."

"I'll have a Heineken."

As the bartender drew the beer, he continued to stare at Bill with a puzzled expression.

"Are you Bill Sanders?"

"Yes. Do we know each other?"

"I recognized you from your picture in Saturday's paper. We were in the same class at Jefferson High. I'm Jim Gassert."

"Of course!" They shook hands.

His memory jogged, Bill could now see within Jim's older face the youngster he remembered.

"You were in *Hamlet* with me and Paul Watson."

"Sure was. I was Laertes. You were Claudius and Paul was Hamlet. I'm not sure we covered ourselves with theatrical glory, but at least we didn't blow any lines. Not that I remember anyway."

The mention of Paul caused them both to pause. Jim cleared his throat. Bill took a sip of beer.

"That was terrible what happened to Paul last year. I was on a road trip and couldn't make it to his funeral. They never have found his daughter."

"I know. I was talking to Dave Taylor at lunch, and he said they were at a dead end on both Cindy's case and Daniel Scott's murder."

"So, the Courier says you're in town to help that director decide if he wants to shoot a movie of your novel here."

"Yes, but I don't know much more than that. The director's arriving later today."

"Well, I hope it works out. It sure would help my business."

"You own this place? What happened to Ralph Singer?"

"Oh, he's been dead about ten years now. Cancer. After he died, a couple of his nephews took over the Oasis and tried to run it. But they couldn't get along. Or rather their wives couldn't get along. Anyway, they wound up filing for bankruptcy a couple of years ago. The place sat empty until I bought it about six months ago. I was working for the state in Indianapolis and really wanted to move back to Jefferson. I was able to take early retirement and made a low-ball bid on the property and got it. Business has been pretty good. Especially at nights and on the weekends. We added some booths, a couple of tables, and a small kitchen in the back so we could offer some food in addition to booze. Hamburgers, fries, and sandwiches mostly. I have a couple of full-time bartenders and two servers. The bartenders usually work nights. The server who works the lunch shift called in sick today, but luckily the lunch crowd was small. As you can see, Monday is usually pretty slow."

"Ralph used to serve me beer before I was twenty-one."

"You weren't the only one. But that was back in the day. No more. The state's got real tough on that."

Bill took another sip of beer.

Jim wiped the top of the bar with a wet sponge.

"If I remember right, you weren't born here. Didn't you show up in junior high?"

"Fifth grade. We moved here from across the river in Kentucky when my father was able to buy a small farm not too far out of town."

"Now I remember. Isn't that when you and Paul became best buddies?"

"Sure was. We were best friends through college. After that, even though we stayed in touch, we drifted apart. Paul came back here to be a guidance counselor and I took off for a career in journalism. He called me to come out here last spring to help him search for Cindy. We got nowhere. I was here when Paul was killed."

"You live in New York?"

"Yep, in Manhattan."

"I was there a couple of times on state business. Don't know how you stand it."

"I guess I'm just used to it."

Jim poured himself a glass of water. Bill took another sip of beer.

"Jim, can I ask you a question?"

"Sure. Shoot."

"When I came out here last year to help Paul, I discovered that there had been a number of UFO sightings in and around Jefferson. Mainly from kids who were out later than they should be. Only a few stories appeared in the Courier because Neal thinks the whole subject is just the imagination of kooks and potheads. Some private UFO investigators showed up, but as far as I know nothing came of it."

"I remember. I was still in Indianapolis then, but Jean— my wife, who's not from around here—and I were getting ready to move back here. We wanted to buy a house, so we were looking at the Courier real estate ads online. I remember seeing a couple of very short stories about UFO sightings. I didn't think much of them. Guess I kind of agree with Neal."

"My question is, have you heard any scuttlebutt about UFO sightings? After all, where better to pick up gossip than the town's most popular bar? I'll check back issues of the paper later at the Courier office. Or maybe online, given Neal's touchiness on the subject."

"Well, I don't remember any more stories in the paper, but I could have missed them. But, sure, I've heard talk in the bar about UFOs. I didn't pay much attention. A couple of guys said they saw strange lights over the river late at night. Oh, I just remembered—I think it was last month—Bob Nelson said his wife took their dog out for a walk a little after midnight and came back shaken and very upset. Said she had seen a triangle of thee big lights in the sky and the space between the lights blocked out the stars. Whatever that means. Bob almost got laughed out of the place. Everybody wanted to know what his wife had been drinking. But he swore she was telling the truth. Why are you interested in UFOs?"

"No reason, really. Just curious, I guess. Seems like a lot of sightings for a small town."

"Could be a lot of copycat stories. Somebody sees a helicopter, thinks it's a UFO. And it goes from there."

Bill drank the last of his beer.

"You're probably right. How much do I owe you?"

"It's on the house. Just get that movie made here."

"Thanks. I'll do my best."

CHAPTER 4

It was after three when Bill started walking back to the hotel. Despite the chilly wind, the heavy lunch followed by a beer made him a little sleepy. His mind drifted and he began to think more about events stemming from his trip to Jefferson last year to help Paul.

After the murders of Daniel Scott and Paul, I called Warren Holden, who had strong ties to the intelligence community. I told him everything I knew up to that point. He advised me to talk to Walter Jansen, a former aide to Jimmy Carter who works at the Carter Center and has an interest in unidentified flying objects. Jansen was with Carter in 1969 when the soon-to-be governor of Georgia claimed to have seen a UFO. Operatives of The Seven caused truck fires on a bridge in Louisville to stop me from flying to Atlanta to meet Jansen. I learned from a radio news report that Holden, who I felt was holding something back when we talked, had died of a "heart attack." Believing he was murdered, and mindful of the threatening note I found in my duffel, I fled Jefferson for New York. Soon after arriving, I got a FedEx envelope from Holden, sent the day before he died, containing a piece of paper with the name COL. (RET.) RICHARD WEST in handwritten block letters. That was the real beginning. But of what?

Bill walked across the hotel lobby. It was empty. No sign of Steve at the front desk. No Monday afternoon paper yet. Bill took the elevator to the third floor and room thirty-seven.

He took his shoes off and stretched out on the king-size bed; it didn't take him long to fall asleep.

Bill awoke with a start. For a few seconds he was confused, not sure where he was. The sight of his duffel bag focused his mind. The room was semi-dark. He glanced at his watch. Six-thirty. Jack Turner should be arriving any time. He looked at his cell phone. No missed calls.

He had just returned the phone to the bedside table when it started chirping. *I've got to get someone who knows how to help me change that ring tone.*

"Hello."

"Bill Sanders?"

"Yes."

"It's Jack Turner. Joan and I just got off the plane and are getting ready to drive to the hotel. Someone at the airport said it only takes about fifteen minutes."

"If that. I'm here. Room thirty-seven. Just give me a call or knock on the door when you get checked in."

"Great. I'm really looking forward to meeting the author of *Look Down.*"

"And I'm looking forward to meeting the director of the movie."

"I think we're going to have a productive week. See you in a bit."

"Okay. Bye."

Bill put on his shoes, splashed some water on his face, combed his hair, and changed shirts.

I wonder what a top Hollywood director, used to lots of glitz and glamour, will think of Jefferson, population eight thousand or so? Who knows? He might like it. Attractive riverfront walks and park. The nineteenth-century Neo-Classical and Federal-style buildings in the old part of town that have been carefully preserved, partly out of civic pride and partly to attract tourists looking for a dose of nostalgia. A population that has remained stable over the years. Jefferson was never a bedroom community for a larger city; it exists on its own terms with an economy based on farming, tourism and some light manu-facturing. I always thought it was a great place for Paul, Jim Gassert, the members of our high school class, and me to grow up. Was it? Is it still?

✳

The knock on the door was loud and strong.

Bill's concept of Hollywood glitz and glamour quickly dissipated when he opened the door. Jack Turner, who appeared to be in his late sixties, was slightly shorter than Bill. He had close-trimmed gray hair, heavy jowls, and red-rimmed droopy eyes. He was wearing blue jeans, scuffed brown loafers, and a red and white striped rugby shirt. Bill had only seen news photos and television images of him, usually in a tuxedo and looking much taller.

Turner stuck out his right hand.

"Hi Bill. Jack Turner."

Bill grasped the outstretched hand.

"Good to meet you. Come in."

"Thanks. Joan will be along in a few minutes. Our rooms are on this floor, just down the hall."

Bill offered the sofa to Turner, taking the wingback chair for himself.

"Nancy Luke predicted you and I would get along just fine."

"Then we will. I've known Nancy for years. I think I was a little in love with her at one point, before she married that rich lawyer. You're lucky as hell to have her for an agent."

"I couldn't agree more."

"She knows how to represent her clients' interests. When she suggested I double your consulting fee, I knew better than to argue with her. That might have caused it to triple. By the way, she's the only person I know who calls me Jack. Everybody else calls me Turner."

"That's fine by me, Turner. I go by Bill."

"Good. Now, Bill, first things first. What about dinner? We had lunch before we left L.A., so we're not starving."

"Neither am I. I had a big lunch around noon. There's a bar a few blocks down the street that's been here for decades. It has a new owner, a guy I went to high school with. I had a beer there after lunch. They serve hamburgers and sandwiches. I've never eaten there, but I imagine it's good enough. Otherwise, there are several restaurants in town, including a couple of pretty fancy ones. At least for these parts."

There was a quiet knock on the door.

"That'll be Joan."

Bill opened the door. And stared. A stunningly beautiful woman with long black hair and intense green eyes looked back at him. She was wearing black slacks, sneakers, and a red sweater. She couldn't have been more than thirty. She offered her hand.

"Hi. You must be Bill Sanders. I'm Joan Wilson, Turner's assistant. What a pleasure to meet you."

Bill took her hand.

"The pleasure is mine. Please come in. We were just discussing where to have dinner."

Turner and Joan agreed that the Oasis would be perfect. They both thought it would help give them a feel for Jefferson.

Turner raised his hand as though he had forgotten something.

"When I checked in, I had a note from the local newspaper editor—I think his last name is Neal—inviting us to dinner at his house tomorrow night. He said it would be just the three of us with him, a reporter, and his wife. What's the deal on that?"

"His name is Graham Neal. Everybody calls him Neal. A fellow last-name guy. His paper is the Jefferson Courier. He told me earlier today he was going to invite you. I know him. I hope you'll accept."

"Of course. It'll help me get to know and understand Jefferson better. Can you RSVP for us?"

"Sure. No problem. I'll e-mail him tonight or call him in the morning. By the way, have you seen Saturday's Courier? Or today's?"

"No. Should I have?"

"Well, Neal heard a rumor that you were coming to town and were seriously considering Jefferson for the movie. He called me Friday in New York and I confirmed it. He had a story Saturday and another one today, which I haven't seen yet. I hope I didn't spill any secrets you were trying to keep. Nancy Luke didn't say anything about keeping a lid on it."

"God, no. Trying to keep secrets in this business is like trying to hold the tide back. I try to be as open as possible. Sometimes I get in trouble for it, but less trouble than if I try to conceal something. Especially something as innocuous as where we're going to shoot a film."

"That's a relief to know."

"Good. Let's go eat."

"I was walking around town today. It's a little chilly outside. Let's drive."

As they walked through the lobby, Bill stopped at the front desk and glanced at the Monday afternoon Courier. Neal was right. Another thin story. There was a two-column shot of Bill walking off the studio jet. And several pictures of locals with short quotes about what they thought of a major motion picture being filmed in Jefferson. Money seemed to be the common theme in their responses.

The three had hamburgers, fries and beer for dinner. They sat at one of the tables in the back of the bar.

"Good choice," Turner said as he popped a French fry into his mouth.

"I agree," Joan added, raising her beer mug in a toast.

Jim Gassert had left for the day when they arrived. Bill didn't know the bartender and server. Both appeared to be in their twenties.

"Turner, before we get down to business, I have a favor to ask."

"What's that?"

"It's about Graham Neal. His family has owned the local paper for nearly a hundred years. It's where I had my first reporting job. He taught me a lot. He's an old friend and a hell of a good guy. I promised him I would try to persuade you to give him and the reporter he's assigned to cover you—his name is John King—some special considerations in terms of news and interviews. They're going to have a lot of competition from the regional and national press, especially if you end up picking Jefferson."

"Oh, sure. Don't worry. Whenever I do a location shoot, I always try to be as accommodating as possible to the local press. Especially if I get invited to dinner."

Joan smiled and gently turned the conversation toward their plans for the week ahead. She pulled a notebook and pen out of her handbag.

"Bill, if you don't mind, I like to write stuff down, so we don't forget something. It also helps keep me focused."

"Not at all. You're talking to an old reporter. I might do the same thing."

Bill drained his beer mug and looked at Turner.

"What's the plan? What do we do tomorrow?"

"The first thing I'd like to do is take a look at the farm where you lived as a kid. That's an important part of the background of the main character in *Look Down*."

"Too late. That farm was turned into a subdivision some years ago."

"Is there a similar farm we could look at?"

"I'm sure there is. We'll just have to drive around until something strikes our fancy."

"I also want to see where you went to grade school and middle school and high school. I want to see a bridge over a creek where we can shoot the scene in which Joseph's pet rabbits are drowned by his father. That didn't really happen, did it?"

"No. It's an autobiographical coming-of-age novel, but still a novel. Fiction."

"Well, it's a powerful scene in the book and will be in the film. Along with the scene where Joseph's brother commits suicide. Fiction again?"

"Yes, I had a younger brother. But he didn't kill himself.

In fact, he died in a prison fight in Texas, where he was serving a life sentence for murder."

"I'm sorry."

"That's okay. It was a long time ago. We weren't close."

Joan interrupted.

"Look, guys. It's well after nine. Obviously, we need to spend the next couple of days driving around with a copy of the screenplay and try to match the main scenes with locations. But we've been going strong since early this morning. Let's call it a night and get a fresh start in the morning."

Turner, whose eyes were a bit redder and droopier, nodded.

The next day the weather turned clear and warmer with only a gentle breeze. Bill, Turner, and Joan spent most of the day driving around Jefferson and Madison County in Bill's rental Buick. Bill volunteered to drive because he knew his way around. Turner sat in the front passenger seat, Joan behind him in the right rear seat. She had highlighted specific scenes in the *Look Down* screenplay for which they tried to find good locations. They first checked out an elementary school on Main Street as well as the high school near the river. Turner liked them both. Joan took pictures with a small, expensive-looking camera she carried in her handbag.

Because there would be some interior scenes at the high school, Turner insisted on doing a walk-through of the building. Bill wished they had been able to give the principal some advance warning, but he was happy to oblige. Bill hadn't been in the building since he was a young reporter during the summers of his college years. He was amazed at how much the place had changed—and how much it hadn't. Despite computers, iPads, and modern desks, the rooms and walls and floors still looked pretty much the same. The smell of oiled wood permeated the air. As they walked past classrooms, students and teachers glanced at them but quickly returned to whatever they were doing or discussing.

Turner stuck his head into an empty classroom. "We'll have to make one of these rooms like it was when Joseph was a student here more than thirty years ago. But that shouldn't be a problem. Not with this old building."

Joan nodded and scribbled in her notebook.

The principal looked puzzled. "Who's Joseph?"

"He's the main character in my novel *Look Down*."

"Oh, of course. Sorry. Will the movie also be called *Look Down*?"

Turner looked a little annoyed. "Certainly. That book's been on the best-seller list forever. We'd be crazy to call the film something else."

The principal stiffened a bit. "Of course, you would have to get the school board's permission to film inside the school."

"That shouldn't be a problem. Plus, if we decide to film here, we could probably use you as an extra in a couple of scenes. That is, if you would agree."

The principal relaxed and grinned. "That would be great."

Bill smiled to himself. *Don't be fooled by the blue jeans and scuffed shoes. He's a smooth operator.*

Next, they drove out of town to look for a farm that might work. Before Bill realized it, they were coming up to the culvert where The Seven's helicopter had forced Paul to crash his Jeep. He felt a lump in his throat. *Jesus, why did I come this way?*

A mile or so past the crash site, Turner motioned to Bill to pull over and stop the car at the beginning of a gravel lane leading down a gentle hill to a small farm.

"This place looks perfect. The house. The barn. The silo. They're just right. Do you know who lives here?"

"Don't have a clue. The name Pearson is on the mailbox. Do you want to pull in and see if someone's home?"

"No. We shouldn't talk to them until we've made a decision. Make a note, Joan, so we can get back to them later."

Joan scribbled in her notebook and then took a picture of the farm.

Since they had eaten a big breakfast at the hotel and were

going to Neal's for dinner, they decided to skip lunch.

As Bill was turning the car around, Turner started to say something, but paused as another car pulled up beside theirs.

The driver and passenger both got out. Bill recognized the passenger as Jeff Keefer, the photographer he met at Jefferson Field.

Bill lowered his window.

"Hi. I'm John King from the Courier. This is Jeff Keefer, our photographer. Mind if we tag along?"

Bill looked at Turner.

"Fine by me. Any objections, Joan?"

"Nope."

After introductions and handshakes all around, the two-car caravan headed back toward town.

Turner turned to Bill.

"I was starting to ask if you've thought anymore about a good spot for the scene in which Joseph's father drowns the rabbits?"

"Well, there's a state park on the other side of town that has a creek flowing through it that eventually empties into the Ohio River. There are several wooden footbridges over the creek that were built by the WPA in the nineteen-thirties. One of those might work."

"Sounds good. Let's go look."

"We'll have to walk to get to the bridges. Might be muddy."

"No problem for me. Joan?"

"Nope. That's why I wore sneakers."

Once inside the park, they had to walk only a few hundred yards to see two of the bridges. The walking paths were covered with fine gravel, so there was no mud. Jeff Keefer took several pictures; John King asked a few questions and scribbled notes into a reporter's notebook. His questions indicated he had read *Look Down*.

Turner liked both sites. Joan photographed them.

"Either one of these is perfect. I don't need to see more."

At a stoplight outside the park, Bill turned to Turner.

"Why did Chris Wade have Joseph's brother hang himself

in the screenplay when in the book he takes a big overdose of sleeping pills?"

"I don't really know, but I expect Chris thought hanging would be more filmic. I like it better. It should take place inside the barn. As I remember the book, the kid was in the basement of the family's farmhouse when he swallowed the pills. What works on a printed page and what works in a film can be very different animals."

Bill's cell phone chirped. It was John King.

"Mr. Sanders, I think we have enough. We're going to head back to the office. Thanks to you and Mr. Turner for your co-operation. I'll see you at dinner tonight at Neal's house."

"Good. It was a pleasure to meet you. See you later."

"Bye."

"That was John King, the reporter. Neal must have given him my phone number. They're headed back to the Courier."

Joan put her notebook away and cleared her throat.

"Okay, guys. It's almost three. I suggest we head back to the hotel, so we have time to rest a bit before dinner tonight. We're invited for seven. What's the protocol here? On time? Or fashionably late?"

"I haven't lived here since I was a kid, but I think on time is a safe bet."

When Bill pulled into the hotel parking lot, Turner let out a groan. There were two TV vans and several cars parked hap-hazardly. The logo on one van was for a TV station in Louisville. The other van was from an Indianapolis station. One of the cars had Ohio license plates.

"The circus is starting. These TV guys are from Louisville and Indianapolis. There may be a print reporter from the Cincinnati paper. The national media won't be far behind. Turner, I hope you remember your promise to me about Gra-ham Neal and the Courier."

"Don't worry."

Once they entered the lobby, several reporters and two cameramen crowded around, peppering them with questions.

Turner was very soft-spoken and polite. He would only say that he was considering Jefferson for the filming of *Look Down*, but nothing had been decided. He said there were at least three other locations under consideration, but he declined to name them.

One of the TV reporters asked Bill if he wanted his book filmed in Jefferson.

"I think that would be great, but it's not my decision."

Turner raised his hand.

"Ladies and gentlemen, that's it for today. We may have an announcement later in the week. Right now, I'm going to take a nap."

Dinner was a great success. Neal lived in a riverfront mansion that had been built by his grandfather. Marge, who visited a cousin in London for several weeks every other year or so, had decorated the house, from slipcovers to china, with an English flair. Cocktails, including Neal's famous martinis, were served in the spacious living room.

Neal and Turner hit it off from the very beginning. Turner had endless questions about Jefferson and its history. Joan and John King discovered a common interest in films from the nineteen-forties. Soon they were comparing favorite lines from *Casablanca*. Marge quizzed Bill about his experiences since leaving Jefferson. She was especially curious about his life in New York.

"I'll never forget my stays in London. The plays. The excitement. It must be like that in New York."

"It can be, but I guess I've been living there for so long that I take a lot of it for granted. I enjoy getting away. Especially since Jane died."

"Oh, Bill. I'm so sorry. I didn't know her, but what a terrible loss it must have been. To have a marriage cut short by such tragedy. How long were you married?"

"Twenty-six years."

The talking stopped when Louise came into the living room from the dining room to announce that dinner was served.

The conversations continued through salads, prime rib with Yorkshire pudding, and strawberries and ice cream for dessert.

Over coffee and brandy, Turner tapped a spoon against his cup.

"Listen up, everyone. I have an announcement. After just one day of scouting around, I've decided we're going to shoot *Look Down* in Jefferson. The town is perfect for the film. I don't need to see more to make a decision. I do want to scout some more locations over the next day or two, but the decision is made."

As everyone applauded, Bill noticed that Joan didn't look the least bit surprised. *Turner must have discussed it with her before we left the hotel for Neal's house. Does he have that kind of authority to make such a major decision on his own, or did he consult with studio brass?*

"And—this is for Neal and John—I'm giving you the story exclusively. Neither I nor the English-Frostmann publicity people will make an announcement until Thursday afternoon. Your paper hits the streets Wednesday afternoon. That gives you a day to own the story. What's your deadline, Neal?" *He must have consulted with the studio.*

"Noon. Paper should be out by three."

"Then I'm yours in the morning for an exclusive interview. I'm pretty certain Bill will agree to join us."

"I will, of course."

"How about if Bill and I come to your office at eight in the morning? I'd like to bring Joan along to take notes and remind me if I forget something. Does that give you enough time to interview us and and get the story written?"

"I think so. John, you're going to write it. If the interview takes an hour or so, can you have the story together in two hours? We need to leave a little time for me to edit it."

"Shouldn't be a problem. I'll type fast."

Turner smiled.

"Great. The only thing we can't talk about is who will star in the film. The studio has just started casting, and these negotiations are delicate. All I can say at this point is that you won't be disappointed. Filming will start in late August or September, assuming all the legal stuff can be worked out and the city and county governments agree to let us generate mayhem and block traffic. We'll also need to hire lots of locals as extras."

Neal smiled.

"I expect no problems. You and English-Frostmann will be very welcome in Jefferson."

After dinner, Joan and John King went to the Oasis for some more drinks and film talk. Bill and Turner returned to the hotel, where they sat in the lobby to talk for a few minutes.

"That was really good of you to set up the interview for tomorrow with Neal and John."

"In my situation, it's really important to get on the good side of the local press. Besides, it doesn't cost me much. The national media might be irked for a day or two, but they'll get over it. The truth is they don't care much about what the local press does. They know it'll stay local. Neal and John will look great to their readers for getting a big story first. But when it's reported nationally, no one outside Jefferson will know or care about the Courier's 'scoop.' That's cynical, I know, but accurate. No one should know that better than you."

"True. I remember years ago when I worked for The Louisville Courier-Journal, which is not exactly a small-town paper, I did a story on an Indiana University archeologist who had made an important find in a cave in Greece. About a week later, The New York Times ran a very similar story by one of its reporters that made no mention of my Courier-Journal story. As far as national readers knew, the Times broke the story."

"My point exactly."

"I wanted to ask you something that may seem nosey. If you think it is, just say so. It has to do with my ignorance of the movie business."

"Fire away. I know how to say 'no comment.'"

"At dinner tonight you said you had decided on shooting the film here. Were you able to make that decision on your own, or did you have to consult with English-Frostmann executives? You also said the studio would hold its publicity machine in check until a day after tomorrow's Courier is printed. Were you able to give that order or did you have to get approval from someone higher up?"

"Good questions. The truth is, as long as I don't blow the budget too badly, I have almost total autonomy over *Look Down*. That's because of a string of successes for the studio and three Academy Awards. Plus, the intangible mystique that comes from media bullshit, like dubbing me 'Mr. Hollywood.' The decisions were mine. I discuss things with the studio brass, but they always go along because they trust me. They're also afraid I might go to another studio in the future if I don't get my way."

"Thanks for the education."

"My pleasure. I'm ready for bed. No telling when Joan and John will return. They have youth on their side. After we talk to Neal and John in the morning, let's drive around some more and look at other possible locations."

"Sounds good."

CHAPTER 5

Bill and Morgen were again at the airliner crash site near JFK. Only now things looked different. It was darker and long shadows obscured much of what was going on. The secretive men in the third crop row were still doing something that they were covering with green sheets. A few rescue workers were milling around, but there were no more stretchers or bodies. Bill grabbed one of the workers by the arm.

"Where the hell are the bodies? Where's my wife? I saw her here earlier and she was alive. She blinked at me!"

"There were no survivors." After uttering those four words, the worker looked at Bill, grinned, and disappeared into thin air.

Bill was flabbergasted; Morgen seemed unconcerned.

Bill walked over to the third row, grabbed one of the white-coated men by the sleeve, and demanded to know what he was doing.

"I can't talk to you, Sir. You're not allowed to be in this area. You were warned by your guide."

Bill took a step back and bumped into Morgen, who took his hand.

"Let's get out of here."

"I can't. I have to find Jane. I know she's here and alive."

"Bill, you have to let Jane go. She's dead."

Bill began to cry.

Another white-coated man, bald and much taller than the first, approached them.

"Follow me. I will show you the truth you seem to yearn for."

He took Bill and Morgen past the third crop row, where there was a large trench. It was full of what at first looked like dolls. On looking closer, Bill realized they were adults who had somehow been shrunken to less than a foot in height. One of them was Jane, but now her eyes were closed.

"She was alive earlier. What have you done? Did you kill her? Why have you shrunk these people?"

"You have an overactive imagination, Sir. She was killed in the crash. She must be treated the same as the others. It's the law. It's always been thus."

With that, all the men in white coats suddenly vanished like the rescue worker. The tiny bodies in the trench were also gone, replaced by the full-sized body of Paul Watson!

Morgen stifled a scream and squeezed Bill's hand.

"Who's that?"

"Paul Watson. My boyhood friend who was killed in Indiana."

As Bill and Morgen stared down at him, Paul opened his eyes and sat upright. He reached inside his green flannel shirt, pulled out a notebook, and silently held it out to Bill.

Bill reached out to take the notebook just as it and Paul disappeared.

Now alone at the crash site, Bill and Morgen were surrounded by pieces of the wrecked jetliner. There were no other people. No sign of their driver or his car. It was growing dark and cold. There was a strange double light blinking in the distance. They decided to walk toward it, shivering and hugging each other for warmth ....

Bill jerked awake in a cold sweat. He was hugging a pillow and his legs were twisted in the top sheet and blanket. Two neon signs down the street were blinking through his window. He looked at his watch. Four-thirty. Wednesday. He lay back and tried to calm down.

Another weird dream. With Morgen and Jane. And Paul Watson! Why were Jane and the other victims the size of dolls? What did it mean that she must be treated the same as the others? Why did everyone disappear, including Paul just as he was trying to hand a notebook to me?

A notebook? Sharon mentioned a notebook the last time we talked, when she became hysterical and blamed me for Paul's death. She said she had found snippets of writing in a notebook in Paul's desk that showed he had told me the UFO story. And also, that I knew he told her and Dave Taylor.

A notebook. Paul was trying to hand me a notebook. Is there something else in it? Is it still in his desk? If there is more, did Sharon read it? Or did she become hysterical and stop as soon as she learned I knew about Paul's UFO account? I know enough about dreams to know that all the characters in a dream are usually some aspect of the dreamer. Was my subconscious reminding me of the notebook Sharon mentioned? If so, why?

Bill clicked on his bedside light, picked up his wallet, and got out of bed. He walked across the room to a closet where he had stashed his backpack and found the key to Paul's house. He carefully put the key in an inside compartment of his wallet.

The interviews in Neal's office went smoothly. Both Neal and John King were especially interested in the logistics of bringing Hollywood to Jefferson. How many people would be involved? How many trucks and how much equipment would be moving into Jefferson? How long would they stay? Where would they stay? Does the town have enough hotels and motels? Would streets need to be blocked off? How would all these extra workers and actors be fed? How many locals would be hired as extras? How much would they be paid? How and where can residents apply to be extras?

Neal asked Bill if he planned to be in Jefferson during the filming.

"I'm not sure. I'm in the middle of a major book project and by then will be busy writing. But if I can possibly break away, I'll try to come out for at least a few days. I'd like to meet the actors, especially whoever the two are who play Joseph as a child and as an adult. This is my first time dealing with Hollywood, so I'm curious and I guess a little starstruck."

Neal chuckled.

"Aren't we all?"

After the interviews, Bill, Turner, and Joan grabbed a quick lunch at the Jefferson Cafe. Bill was relieved that Dave Taylor didn't show up.

The three spent the afternoon looking at more sites. Joan made notes and took more photographs.

They were turning into the hotel parking lot when Turner reached over and touched Bill's arm.

"I've seen enough. This town is perfect. I don't need to see anymore. I want to go back to L.A. tomorrow so I can be there when the studio makes the official announcement. Joan, can you arrange for the plane to pick us up at eight in the morning? Bill, do want to return to New York tomorrow afternoon? We'll send the plane back for you."

"No. I'd like to stay until Saturday. I can take a commercial flight back home from Louisville."

"No way. We made a deal. Joan, arrange for the plane to return to Jefferson on Saturday to take Bill to New York. What time, Bill?"

"Noon, I guess."

"Done. Just be at that little airport then. Now, let's take a break and then go back to that bar—What's it called? The Oasis?—for some dinner. I liked that place. Great French fries. Does that suit you, Bill? Joan?"

Both nodded.

Inside the lobby was a stack of papers. A huge headline and subhead were spread across the top of the front page:

HOLLYWOOD HEADED TO JEFFERSON
Major Studio Will Film Sanders Book Here

Next to the story was a three-column picture of Turner, Bill, and Joan looking at the footbridge at the state park. Inside were more pictures of Bill and Turner.

When he got to his third-floor room, Bill kicked his shoes off and stretched out on the bed to read the paper. He was impressed with John King's graceful writing style, as well as the questions and answers he emphasized. He's got a future in the business, Bill thought, then felt a pang of sadness for Daniel Scott. He had a future, too. Until he was killed by the United States Government for doing his job.

What a fucking mess! I wish Warren Holden had never given me Colonel Richard West's name. But then I never would have known Morgen Remley. After my meeting with West, I'll probably never see her or hear from her again.

His mind drifted back to his first encounter with Morgen when she introduced herself to him in the main branch of the New York Public Library on Fifth Avenue. Bill had just returned to New York from Jefferson. He was at the library searching for information on Colonel West. They hit it off, and Bill hired her to help him get to the bottom of the strange events in Jefferson. Morgen was a pretty blonde, thirty-one years old, with a doctorate in marine biology. She told Bill she was also a part-time researcher for MUFON, and she gave him a crash course in UFOs and alien abductions before they started searching in earnest for the mysterious Colonel West. The search took them to Washington and then to Belgium, where West had served with NATO a decade earlier. The closest they could come to tracking him down was a letter he had sent to a friend in Brussels almost nine years ago. The return address was a post office box in Pine Bush, New York. Both Bill and Morgen recognized Pine Bush as a UFO hot spot and suspected that such a coincidence might somehow link West to events in Jefferson. But they realized that a nine-year-old trail was pretty cold. Especially from someone as secretive as Colonel West. While in Belgium, Bill and Morgen became lovers, despite their age difference; Bill realized he had loved Morgen from the first time they met. They returned to New York, unsure if it was worthwhile to look for Colonel West in Pine Bush.

It was then that Colonel West called Bill and arranged for the three of them to meet under extraordinary circumstances.

CHAPTER 6

After seeing Turner and Joan off at the airport, Bill returned to the hotel. He needed time to be alone and think.

Paul's notebook. In their final conversation, Sharon said she had found it in Paul's desk. She must have meant the small desk in the den that was between the two upstairs bedrooms; one bedroom was Paul's and Sharon's and the other Cindy's.

Was the notebook still there or did Sharon take it with her to Indianapolis?

Bill decided to look for the notebook. He had Paul's house key in his wallet, if Sharon hadn't changed the locks. If Neal's theory was right that Sharon was keeping the house so Cindy would have a familiar place to return to, then it wouldn't have made sense to change the locks. Paul hadn't changed locks after the break-in last year. The front-door lock had been picked. Changing it wouldn't have made it less pickable.

At first, Bill figured he would go to the house after dark. *No. That would be dumb. I would have to turn on some lights or use a flashlight. Either might attract attention. And what if the night deputy happened to check on the house while I was prowling around in the dark? Better to go in the middle of the day. It'll look more like I belong there, not like I'm sneaking around.*

Bill left the hotel and started for Paul's house shortly before eleven. The day was cool and sunny with only a few clouds in the sky.

When Bill pulled into Paul's gravel driveway, the clearing

in front of the two-story log house was bathed in shadows from the surrounding trees. The clearing became even darker as a cloud suddenly passed in front of the sun. A feeling of foreboding passed over Bill; he sat in the car and tried to shake it off. He looked at the sky above the roof of the house and remembered segments of Paul's account last spring of what happened the night Cindy vanished.

As I started to turn down our lane, I noticed lights over the house. They seemed to pulsate, red and green and white. My first thought was that it was a helicopter, but there wasn't any noise. The whole house was bathed in light. When my eyes adjusted a little to the brightness, I looked up and that's when I saw it. A big goddamn machine shaped like a triangle, bigger than the house or the clearing, was just hanging there in the sky about a hundred feet over the roof.

I was scared shitless. I jumped out of the car and started to run toward the front door, screaming for Sharon. Before I could get five steps, I was hit by some kind of electricity. I fell on my back unable to move or make a sound. But I could still see the machine and the east side of the house, where Cindy's room is upstairs. Then I noticed a blue beam of light about two feet wide running from the machine, or whatever the hell it was, to Cindy's window. Cindy was floating inside that beam of blue light, in the air, between her window and the object. I could see her clearly. She was asleep in her green pajamas, her arms at her side.

I must have passed out, because when I awoke about fifteen or twenty minutes later everything appeared normal. I could move, although I felt stiff and sick to my stomach, and dazed. It was about twenty minutes past midnight. I ran into the house screaming for Cindy and Sharon. Cindy's bed was empty, and Sharon was sound asleep. But she was sleeping like she was drugged. I had a hard time waking her up and when she did get up, she was confused and groggy. There was a funny smell in the house, kind of like burned cinnamon, but it was gone in a few minutes. We searched the house and yard. We even looked into the edge of the woods and out on the road before we called Dave's office. He and his deputies also searched the house and the yard, as well as the woods.

It was then that Paul revealed two things to Bill that he

hadn't told anyone—not Sharon or the Sheriff. *When Cindy was in that blue light, she wasn't being pulled from her window. She was floating toward the window. And just before I passed out, I heard something in the distance: the heavy thumping sound of a helicopter.*

Bill had been more confused than ever, both about Paul's account and his mental state, when he heard that Cindy was apparently being returned to her room and there was a helicopter in the distance. If Cindy was being returned, where was she? Could the helicopter be what Paul, who had been drinking, had seen all along? But what was a helicopter doing over Paul's house in the middle of the night?

It was only after Bill's meeting with Colonel West that these two elements of Paul's account made sense. Too late for Paul to know.

Bill finally got out of the car and walked up to the front door of the house. The key unlocked the door without a hitch.

Inside, things looked much the same as last year except for a thin layer of dust. Bill stepped into the kitchen and picked up the phone. No dial tone. Disconnected. The refrigerator was unplugged, and its doors were propped open with rubber wedges.

The door to the guest room where he had slept was open. It looked the same; the bed was neatly made.

Bill climbed the stairs to the two upstairs bedrooms. Both doors were closed. He went directly to the small den between them and sat down at Paul's wooden desk. No computer was in sight. *Sharon probably took it with her to Indianapolis.* There was a center drawer and three vertical drawers to the right. None were locked.

Bill pulled open the center drawer. Among pencils, pens, and paper clips was a small spiral notebook. He put it on the desktop and looked at the first page. There, in Paul's cramped handwriting, were two sentences: *I have told Bill about the UFO and that I also told Sharon and Dave. Bill doesn't believe me, but he has agreed to help me search for Cindy.* The rest of the notebook pages were blank.

Bill was confused. This was clearly the notebook entry that had set Sharon off in their last telephone conversation. But why did Paul write down such a snippet? He must have written it when Bill left him at the house to go into town to see Dave and Neal. Sharon was long gone by then and didn't return until after Paul was killed. Did he want her to find it later? Was it a note to himself? For what? Bill's powerful dream of Paul trying to hand him a notebook seemed to imply more than these two sentences stating what Bill obviously knew. Maybe it, or the dream, meant nothing.

Bill pushed the notebook aside and opened the top drawer on the right. It contained a stapler, some boxes of staples and paper clips, and a small digital camera. Bill picked up the camera and turned it on. There were only two pictures, both of Cindy sitting on her bed in her pajamas. The images were almost two years old, according to the date imprinted on a corner of each picture.

The second drawer was crammed full of computer cables, extension cords, and old electronic gear.

The bottom drawer contained a stack of files full of tests, booklets, surveys and other material presumably related to Paul's counseling work at the high school. One of the files in the middle of the pile was thicker than the rest. Bill pulled it out, and another spiral notebook fell out onto the floor. Bill leaned over and picked it up. It was bigger than the one he had found in the center drawer. A thick rubber band kept the pages together.

Bill slipped the rubber band off the notebook and opened it up flat on the desktop in front of him. There were multiple pages of dated entries in Paul's handwriting. The dates were all during a one-week period last year after Cindy's disappearance and before Bill's arrival in Jefferson. The date at the top of each page was followed by an entry that ended on that page. Sometimes there were two or three consecutive pages with the same date at the top of each. Evidently Paul wrote them at different times during the same day.

The earliest entry was first. It was dated almost a week after Cindy vanished.

Sharon was hysterical after I told her about the UFO the next morning. She screamed that I was crazy and hit me over and over again with her fists. She finally calmed down enough to help in the investigation. But she wouldn't talk to me. She insisted I sleep in the guest room downstairs. Within a week she called her parents to drive down from Indianapolis and pick her up. They came and I haven't seen her or talked to her since. She won't take my calls. Before she left, she said she was too embarrassed to tell her parents about the UFO. But they are more than icy with me. Maybe they think I had something to do with Cindy's disappearance, but Dave cleared me before Sharon left. He checked with the people I had been drinking with that night.

I am alone, which is why I called Bill. Thank God he agreed to come.

The next entry was dated the same day, which was a week before Bill arrived.

There are three things I have to tell Bill, and they aren't going to be easy. First, my account of what happened to Cindy, including that it appeared to me she was being returned to her room in the beam of blue light, not being taken away. Second, that I have been drinking heavily lately because it's the only thing that helps the panic attacks I've been having. Third—and this is the hardest of all—I need to explain the reason for the panic attacks. That they are a reaction to sudden memories from my past that have come out of the blue like a thunderbolt for the last year and a half. Some involve UFOs. And alien beings. Some involve Bill. Do the memories have anything to do with Cindy's abduction? Are the aliens keeping it in the family?

Bill's hands were trembling as he read the last few sentences of this entry. Paul was killed before he could tell Bill about the cause of his panic attacks. After his meeting with Colonel West, Bill did not doubt the reality of UFOs and aliens. Now it appeared that Paul was somehow involved with UFOs long before Cindy was abducted. But how was Bill involved?

Bill thumbed through the notebook. There were at least a dozen more pages of entries.

Did Sharon see this notebook, or just the smaller one in the middle drawer? Remembering their last conversation, Bill assumed she had only seen the first one. Otherwise she would have mentioned something about what he had read so far. She probably didn't even know about the bigger notebook, given that it was hidden in the middle of a school-related file. Was this Paul's only diary? Unlike Bill, who as a kid was constantly recording his thoughts and activities, Paul never did so. He sometimes joked about Bill wasting time writing stuff down. Maybe, in anticipation of Bill's arrival, Paul had started what appeared to be his only diary. Maybe it was an effort to organize his thoughts so he could explain events to Bill more clearly.

Bill stood up and looked out the window. Nobody was around. His Buick was clearly visible. He meant it to be so that no one would think he was sneaking around. But maybe he should leave pretty soon and not push his luck.

He put the rubber band around the notebook and stuck it in an inside jacket pocket. He put the file that had contained Paul's notebook back in the lower drawer, being careful that it was in the exact place it had been when he opened the drawer. He then walked through the house, upstairs and down, looking in closets and drawers for more notebooks. There was no attic, but there was a half-basement, which contained a washer and dryer and a storage area. But no notebooks.

He let himself out the front door, carefully locked it, and put the key back into his wallet. He turned the car around and headed back to the Jefferson Hotel. *I've taken something again, like I did when I took the map from Daniel Scott's room. Maybe I'll return this later. Maybe not.*

Back in his hotel room, Bill sat in the wingback chair, took the rubber band off Paul's notebook, and read the first entry again.

Sharon hit Paul with her fists? That doesn't sound like her. Then again, I really didn't know her that well. I remember a coldness about her when she returned for Paul's funeral. And she certainly didn't hold back when she cursed me and blamed me for Paul's death in that final phone call after she had found the small notebook and learned that I knew about the UFO story.

Paul's third entry was dated the day after the first and second entries.

These sudden memories I have are always preceded by an intense, short headache. Sometimes I have two or three memory attacks—I don't know what else to call them—a day. Sometimes I go for several days without any. Sometimes they come in the middle of the night. The headache wakes me up and then I remember something from the past that scares the shit out of me. One really scary thing is when I remember that there are times that I can't remember. Like when I'm a kid and I'm doing something with Bill or my family and there are just blank spaces in my memory of events. Usually for a couple of hours or so. That time is just missing.

But the scariest of all is when I remember being abducted by those strange gray creatures, usually at night but sometimes in broad daylight. This is what I have to tell Bill. These memories are followed by panic attacks that are more severe than the ones following the missing time memories. The only thing that calms me down in either case is a couple of stiff drinks. Or three. Or four. He's going to think I'm crazy. Maybe I am.

Bill put the notebook on the coffee table, stood up, and got a drink of water from the bathroom. *Could these sudden memories followed by panic attacks explain why Paul was driving his Jeep so fast when he was killed? Or why he was passed out on the sofa when I arrived last year? I guess he was telling me the whole story in stages in hopes that I might accept it better than if he hit me with the entire thing all at once. He just never got to finish.*

Bill sat back down and picked up the notebook. The next entry was dated the same day as the previous one. Paul's account was beginning to ramble, maybe the result of his drinking.

I think I was abducted during the missing time but can't remember.

But why do I remember very clearly other times when I was abducted? It's like my memory was erased some of the time and but not other times. And why have I only begun to remember these things, including the missing time, during the last year or so? I certainly didn't remember them when they happened, some when I was just a child. Why do I remember them decades later?

One really vivid memory is when Bill and I were juniors and went on a three-day fishing and camping trip. I remember we didn't catch any fish, ran out of food, and spent the last part of the trip eating baloney and crackers we bought at a country store.

But, following one of these intense headaches, it was the second night of our long-ago camping trip that I remembered vividly. The memory came back while Sharon and Cindy were asleep upstairs; it was late and I had been reading by the fireplace. The minute the headache hit I knew what was coming. These memories are like waking dreams in which I feel sort of paralyzed until they end. I remembered that Bill and I were sleeping on the ground outside our tent because it was a warm night. The campfire had gone cold. There was a full moon. Bill's snoring woke me, and I realized I needed to pee. I noticed a bright light behind a line of trees. At first, I thought it was the moon, but realized the moon was to my back. Suddenly, the light was directly overhead and shining down on me. I ran back to where Bill, who had stopped snoring, was sleeping. I tried to wake him but couldn't. It was like he was drugged. I felt a tingling sensation on the back of my neck, and everything went black. The next thing I remembered was being flat on my back, totally naked, on a metal-looking table that somehow felt soft and warm. I was in a small, round room with walls softly glowing blue. I felt very calm, not bothered at all that I was naked and exposed. Standing next to me were two short—maybe three- or four-feet tall—gray-skinned creatures with long arms and slender, almost elegant, fingers. They had no hair; their eyes were almond-shaped black liquid pools. One of them touched my arm, and I could suddenly hear him (her?) talking to me but inside my head. I was reassured that all was well, and I would not be harmed. I felt even more relaxed and comfortable. I was amazed they "spoke" English. From above somewhere they lowered a rod that was about two feet long over my chest. It began to emit a humming sound and a white light. They passed the rod and light over my body from head to toe. I could feel a pleasant tickling sensation wherever the light hit me.

The next thing I knew I woke up with no memory of anything but a good night's sleep. I was wearing my undershorts and T-shirt. Bill stirred. We started a fire and made some coffee. Bill said we should start fishing as early as possible because that may be when the fish are biting.

Bill remembered that fishing trip vividly. He could remember nothing of that second night except sleeping well, as he usually did in the outdoors. What to make of Paul's account? Did the light that apparently abducted Paul also render Bill unconscious or, at least, unaware? Based on his talk with Colonel West, Bill believed Paul's delayed memory could be an accurate account of what happened that night. The aliens Paul described must be the "grays" the colonel and many other abductees mentioned. Why does Paul have these "memory attacks" and not Bill? Why doesn't Bill remember the light that took Paul? Why Paul? Why Cindy? There must be some genetic link.

Bill read through some other similar accounts of Paul being abducted. Two of them involved Bill. In one case Paul was spending the night at Bill's house. They were sleeping in twin beds in Bill's room when Paul saw a light through the window. The next thing he knew he was on the soft metal table, completely naked.

Only this time I was in a bigger room with other people like me on other tables. Men and women. All naked, which, again, did not upset me. As usual, I felt very calm and relaxed. There were six gray creatures. None of them "talked" to me this time, but one passed the bright, humming rod over my body again. They did the same thing to the others. The next thing I knew Bill's mom was calling us downstairs for breakfast. I remembered nothing except a good night's sleep.

Bill was puzzled that Paul seemed so calm and relaxed during his abduction. He apparently wasn't hurt or harmed in any way, except psychologically. That was certainly not the experience of other abductees Bill had read about when Morgen had given him a crash course on UFOs. He particularly remembered the Travis Walton case. Walton was missing for five days. He said the grays subjected him to several painful medical procedures and tests that left him weak, hungry, dehydrated, and disoriented. The experience terrified him.

Another of Paul's notebook entries describing a memory attack, which also involved Bill, was especially bizarre.

I think we were in the sixth grade when this happened. It was on the playground of the old North Jefferson Elementary School, which has since been torn down. Morning recess was almost over and Bill and I were milling around with the rest of the students. All of a sudden, a breeze came up and the sky got cloudy. I looked up and there was a big, triangular machine coming from behind a cloud. I looked toward Bill and couldn't believe my eyes. He and all the other students and the teachers were silently frozen in place. They were like statues. Some had their mouths open. A couple had been jumping rope and were frozen in mid-air. I started to scream but felt a tingling sensation and the next thing I knew I was standing in a small room, fully clothed, next to one of the gray creatures. I was calm and relaxed, not frightened at all. He or she was holding a green, dimly glowing, translucent ball about half the size of a bowling ball. The alien then reached out and took my right hand, placing it on the glowing ball. I know this sounds looney, but the sensation that followed felt like my body was being drained of energy. I wanted to lie down and sleep. I closed my eyes for a few seconds. When I opened them, I was standing next to Bill on the playground. He was talking to me. Two of the students were jumping rope and laughing. Everything was perfectly normal. As usual, I remembered nothing until many years later. What has been happening to me? Am I somehow responsible for what happened to Cindy?

Bill was stunned. He had no memory of Paul's abductions. And Paul had never told him because he, too, had no memory—until the last year and a half. Yet Bill was involved in the sense that the aliens somehow put him into a deep slumber while they took Paul to their ships or wherever. Or they froze him in time on the playground. A wave of sadness passed over Bill. *Paul was killed before he could talk to me about these memories. It's not fucking fair. Neither was the murder of Cindy and Daniel Scott. Or the betrayal of Morgen. Goddamn Richard West! Goddamn The Seven!*

CHAPTER 7

The President sat at his desk in the Oval Office. He had just finished his weekly lunch with the Vice-President and wanted to be alone for a while. There was nothing on his schedule until a five o'clock reception across Pennsylvania Avenue at Blair House.

A steward brought in a silver tray with a cup of coffee and a small pitcher of cream and a carafe containing more coffee.

"Anything else, Sir?"

"No, that'll be fine. Thanks."

"You're welcome, Sir."

When the steward had left, the President picked up his phone. His secretary immediately answered.

"Yes, Sir?"

"Martha, I don't want to be disturbed for the next hour."

"Of course, Sir."

The President looked across the Oval Office to the left of the fireplace and at a portrait of Thomas Jefferson. In a safe behind the portrait were photographs that the President wasn't supposed to have or know about. Cole Favate, his childhood friend from Ohio and now an Air Force colonel assigned to the Defense Intelligence Agency at the Pentagon, had given them to him last year. He had warned the President to destroy them after looking at them. The photographs proved that NASA had been lying to him and to the public about the face on Mars and the reality of UFOs. *Who else has been lying? The CIA? The NSA? What the hell is going on? I can understand lying to the public even if I don't think it's a great idea in the long term. But lying to me? I'm the goddamn President of the United States.*

The President reached for his phone again.

"Sir?"

"Martha, get me the CIA Director."

"Right away, Sir."

The President then pressed a button beneath the edge of his desk. It was linked to the White House surveillance center and shut down the hidden video cameras and audio recorders that recorded activity in the Oval Office.

"The Director is on the line, Mr. President."

"Hello, Bob. You got time for a chat?"

"For you, always, Mr. President. What's up?"

"Bob, is there anything going on that I should know about but don't? I don't mean the usual war and terrorism stuff. I mean something under the radar, maybe something weird."

"I don't think I know what you mean, Sir."

"Well, in the past few months I've had a feeling something's not right. A hunch, I guess. I occasionally get the impression that some things are being kept from me by someone or some group for reasons I don't understand. Like a shadow. Do you hear any scuttlebutt about strange stuff going on at NASA? What about these sightings of UFOs by our military pilots that were caught on radar? Did we ever get to the bottom of that?"

"Those guys at NASA are up to their usual business. Nothing strange that I know of. The military UFO sightings are still being analyzed. I'll make sure you get a copy of the final report. Mr. President, nobody is keeping anything from you. And, believe me, the UFO thing is a black hole you don't want to fall into. Remember Jimmy Carter? My political advice would be to avoid that topic altogether."

"I've already won my second term. But I guess you're right, Bob. I'm probably reading too much into things. Stress can do that. I'm going up to Camp David this weekend to relax a bit."

"Good idea, Mr. President. Enjoy yourself."

"Thanks, Bob. Bye."

I've known Robert Walker most of my life. We were roommates in college. I could tell from his voice that he was lying to me just now. But about what? And why?

CHAPTER 8

It was early May and spring had finally arrived in New York City when Bill stepped off the Acela train at Penn Station a little past noon. He had spent the remainder of March and most of April in Beirut, Tel Aviv, and Cairo before flying to Washington to finish up a handful of interviews on Capitol Hill and at the State Department. Tired of lugging his old duffel around, he had ditched it in London for a suitcase with wheels. The salesman at Harrods told him it was called a rollaboard. Whatever it was called, it was a lot easier to pull around than his duffel. And he was able to hook his backpack onto the rollaboard's extended handle. *I should have gotten one years ago. Jane always said I was a bit retro, along with secretive. She was right.* He had left the country right after English-Frostmann had announced that Jack Turner would be filming *Look Down* in Jefferson. He left when he did partly to avoid the interviews and publicity. Some enterprising reporters, including an old friend from The New York Times, tracked him down overseas, but most didn't go to the trouble. The Times did a front-page story on Jefferson and the movie. The story was also fodder for the morning network TV shows and popular magazines. The studio had not yet disclosed the names of the actors, which would trigger a second round of publicity.

He hailed a taxi for the ride to Eastside Towers on East Seventy-Second Street. His apartment was on the thirty-second floor and had a commanding southern view of the East River and the United Nations building. He was anxious to be home and off the road.

"Welcome home, Mr. Sanders."

George Carson, the chief doorman at Eastside Towers, grinned and shook Bill's hand before getting his suitcase out of the trunk of the taxi.

"Will you be staying home for a while?"

"I'm finished traveling for the time being. I have a book to write that will take at least a year."

"Well, that's good. I've looked in on your apartment from time to time. Everything's fine. Your cleaning lady was here just last week. I collected your mail. It's on your dining room table."

"Thanks, George." Bill slipped him a fifty-dollar bill.

Once in his apartment and unpacked, Bill realized he was hungry; however, there was virtually no food in the apartment. He was tired of eating in restaurants. He changed into some blue jeans and a sweatshirt and headed out to a small supermarket a couple of blocks away. In thirty minutes, he checked out of the grocery with five bags. He left the groceries at the store and headed home; they would be delivered in less than half an hour. One of the small pleasures of New York life, he thought, as he walked home empty-handed.

Over a ham and onion sandwich and a glass of milk, Bill sorted through the stack of mail George had left. There were two royalty statements from Nancy Luke and three credit card bills, which he had paid online while traveling. The rest was junk mail, including a flyer from the Jefferson Hotel in Indiana reminding him of several summer events in Jefferson, including a music festival and a barbecue cook-off, for which he was invited to make reservations.

Bill had been busy since his March trip to Jefferson to meet Jack Turner and hadn't thought much about events there. But the hotel advertisement brought it all back. It was about a year ago that he got the call for help from Paul. If he had known where that was going to lead, would he have gone to Jefferson?

That's an unfair question to ask myself. Nobody can know the future. I couldn't have refused Paul. And I never would have known and loved Morgen. Morgen, with the blond hair and beautiful blue eyes and musky perfume. Morgen, who loved me and betrayed me. Morgen, who I forgive and will never stop loving.

Bill, lost in thoughts of Morgen, was startled when his doorbell rang.

It was George.

"Mr. Sanders, someone left this on my desk in the lobby. I don't know who or when. I must have been in the restroom or outside hailing a taxi for someone. I sometimes don't go to my desk for hours at a time."

George handed Bill a manila envelope with just his name printed on the front in block letters. The entire envelope was sealed in heavy transparent tape.

"Thanks, George."

Bill's first thought was that the envelope could be a letter bomb. But through the tape he could feel folded paper inside. *Jesus, I've been in the Middle East too long. But why all the tape? To keep someone from opening it and then sealing it back up?*

Bill took the envelope into his office, sat down at his desk, and pulled a pair of scissors from the middle drawer. He cut the end off the taped envelope and pulled out several sheets of expensive, light gray stationery. Printed at the top of each page, in raised black letters, was a name: COL. (RET.) RICHARD WEST. He glanced through the sheets, immediately recognizing the precise cursive he had seen last year on Colonel West's letter to a friend in Brussels.

Bill started to read the first page.

Dear Bill: When you read this, I will have been dead for some time. A trusted friend has promised to see that you get this letter, but not until at least six months after my death. I wanted to give you time to reflect on your experiences and knowledge before I interfered in your life a second time. Please excuse any rambling, inconsistency, or confusion in this letter. I will do my best to be cogent, but I am living now on a heavy dose of pain meds.

Bill stopped reading and put the letter on the top of his

desk. He went into the bathroom and splashed cold water on his face. He felt like he was going to be sick. *This pathological fucker is on my case from beyond the grave. I should not read the letter. I should destroy it.* But he knew there was no way he would ignore the letter or destroy it. It might lead him to Morgen.

Morgen. He thought of the last time he had seen her almost a year ago. It was six in the evening; they were sitting in the back seat of a black U.S. government SUV in front of his apartment building. They were handed hoods to put over their heads and warned not to speak until they were told they could. They were driven by two armed men for almost two hours to somewhere presumably in New York, New Jersey, or Connecticut to meet Colonel West. He had called earlier and set the terms for their meeting.

They ended up at the end of a rutted gravel road; still hooded, they were then led up some stairs and into a building. They were guided into an elevator that took them to a warren of subterranean chambers. Bill and Morgen were separated, and Bill was taken to an office where he was allowed to remove his hood. A few minutes later Colonel West came into the room and introduced himself. He was not a cheerful man. He said he was dying of pancreatic cancer.

The two spent most of the night talking. When they were finished, Bill had learned that UFOs and aliens are a reality; the truth behind events in Jefferson; of the existence of a ultra-secret U.S. government group called The Seven, whose dual goals are to convince the public that the government has secret knowledge of UFOs and is in control of the situation, and to make people who study UFOs the object of ridicule; that Morgen was an agent for The Seven who had betrayed Bill, and he would never see her again unless he agreed to secretly work for The Seven; and that, after he had refused to work for The Seven, he learned that he would keep its secrets or be publicly destroyed by a very convincing file showing him to be an alcoholic drug-user who had been hospitalized several times over the past decade for treatment of paranoid schizophrenia and delusions.

Bill splashed some more water on his face. He realized he could remember almost verbatim snippets of what Colonel West had told him that night.

Cindy Watson is dead. My organization is partly responsible for that. I'll give you the details later.

Before I could step in and get control of the situation, some of our field agents panicked ... and killed Daniel Scott. It might have ended there if you hadn't insisted on a paraffin test. These same agents then killed Paul Watson by forcing his car off the road with a helicopter, as you suspected ... they had concluded he had seen too much and would cause too much trouble. You were next, but the agents ... had enough sense to try to scare you away first. They tried to warn you off with the note they left mentioning your late wife ... that was when they trashed your friend's house in an awkward attempt to cover up the removal of a listening device that they had earlier attached to the phone line. They also smashed your flip phone, hoping that would force you to get a smart phone that would make it easier to track your movements.

Bill remembered the sound of Colonel West's low raspy voice as late night turned into early morning.

Truman appointed an ultra-top-secret panel of seven men to contain and control the growing UFO phenomenon. Rather unimaginatively, they became known as The Seven.

In addition to covering up our almost total lack of knowledge about the aliens, which we have done very successfully, The Seven is also trying to find out what they're up to. Our efforts at this have failed spectacularly.

Only two presidents since Truman—Kennedy and Reagan—and a handful of foreign leaders have known of The Seven's existence.

The bottom line is we don't know anything about UFOs or aliens for certain except that they exist. Not only have aliens been visiting the Earth for thousands of years, they've also established bases on the moon and Mars.

What the government wants to cover up is not what it knows, but what it doesn't know. It's the reverse of the X-Files.

But at the same time the government wants to discredit, mainly through ridicule and disinformation, anyone who has reported UFOs or taken an interest in them.

My main job for The Seven is to oversee the tracking of UFO sightings and abductions. As soon as the aliens release abductees we try to seize them and find out what was done to them. This is what happened to Cindy Watson after she was returned to her room from the UFO. We immobilized her parents with a short-acting sleeping gas; a locksmith's skills made it appear she ran away. But the shock of the original abduction, plus the powerful hypnotic drugs we gave her, proved too much for a ten-year-old. She died, as have some others in similar situations. Her body was cremated at a military base in West Virginia. Her ashes were scattered in a nearby river.

Bill felt a great sadness at the thought of a little girl dying alone or among strangers, her ashes dumped into a cold river far from home. He remembered asking Colonel West two questions: Why not stop killing people and come clean? Why not add UFOs and the aliens to the long list of things we don't understand?

Can you imagine what would happen if we were to confirm that UFO sightings and aliens are real? What if we said to the public: Yes, these craft and beings from we-don't-know-where routinely invade our air space, kidnap our citizens, mutilate our cattle, and we know nothing about the who or the why of any of this. We are powerless, absolutely powerless, to do anything. We don't know whether they are here for good or for evil reasons. And, oh, by the way, we suspect they can read our minds and might be altering our genetic makeup. Can you imagine what would happen to the fabric of society? To religions? To government institutions? To government authority? To the stock market?

It was then that Colonel West stunned Bill with Morgen's betrayal.

Morgen works for The Seven. I'm surprised you haven't figured that out by now. Her assignment was to make contact with you, introduce you a bit to the subject of extraterrestrials and then gently guide you here. All the while she made it seem like your idea. She's very good. She's also a bit of an adventure junkie, which you may have figured out by now. She also likes money, and we pay her well. She makes that story about living on a small inheritance with help from a roommate sound very convincing.

Bill walked back to his office and sat at his desk. He picked up the letter and started to read the rest.

I know you think I am a monster. I sometimes think I am, too. Or that I have become one. I wasn't always the man you saw that night in an underground office. Let me try to explain.

I was recruited to work for The Seven thirteen years ago when the Army stationed me with NATO in Brussels. I was always a good and patriotic soldier, one who obeyed orders without question. It was easy for The Seven recruiters to convince me that working for an ultra-secret government organization would be like an extension of my military service. Only I would have more freedom and authority and a lot more money. I was briefed on the history of The Seven. It was started by Truman in order to help the government get control over a wave of UFO sighting following the end of the Second World War. The reality of UFOs was undeniable. They were flying around in the skies. The government and military knew they could not keep them secret and understandably feared the public would panic. At first, I assumed The Seven wanted to conceal what the government knew about UFOs and aliens. I soon learned the opposite was the case. The Seven was created to cover up the fact that the government doesn't have a clue about UFOs or their occupants. Doesn't know where they're from or what they're doing here. The Seven successfully created the public perception that the government knows way more than it's telling about UFOs and is somehow in league with the aliens to gain access to their advanced technology. At the same time, The Seven made anyone who took UFOs seriously the object of ridicule; as a result, serious scientists avoided the subject like the plague. All those TV shows about coverups of UFOs by the government only helped The Seven's agenda.

But, Bill, you know all this. We discussed it the first and only time we met.

Anyway, I retired and went to work for The Seven. I believed, and still do, that when the group was set up under Truman its aim was positive: prevent a public panic that could be socially and economically catastrophic.

It didn't take long, however, for things to change. And not for the better. The Seven morphed into a self-serving secret empire within the government. A shadow government, if you will, but responsible to no one but itself. It became the victim of too much secrecy, too much money, and too much power. This has happened with secret groups before, but the scope and size of The Seven has no parallel. It took me several years of working for The Seven to realize this. But I was in too deep. I knew too much. I was a loyal soldier. I kept working. My job was to kidnap and study people who had been abducted by UFOs. As you know from the case of your friend's daughter, these people sometimes did not survive our techniques. I had people working for me I couldn't always control. That's why the young reporter and your friend were killed. I couldn't get control over the situation in time. God have mercy on my soul. At least I was able to keep you alive, but it was close. As I explained in our meeting, The Seven had nothing to do with Warren Holden's death; he died of a heart attack. But Holden was aware of The Seven and threatening to expose them. They were going to kill him; his death saved them the trouble.

Remember my telling you that the only two presidents other than Truman who know of The Seven were Kennedy and Reagan? They were both before my time with The Seven, but I was a quick study and had a good ear for scuttlebutt.

Reagan was seriously gaga by his second term. He was easy to control.

Kennedy was another story. When he learned about The Seven, he was furious and formed a super-secret four-man working group in the White House to investigate them. He apparently didn't buy all the studies that said society and the economy would collapse if people learned that UFOs and aliens were real and had been around for centuries. One bit of pervasive gossip was that JFK was set to address the nation, expose The Seven, and cut off the group's funding when he returned to Washington from Dallas in November 1963. I have no proof, but I believe The Seven was the hidden hand behind his assassination. I also have reason to believe that the four members of his working group were warned to disband and never speak of The Seven again or they would face the same fate as their leader.

I also learned that Jimmy Carter was almost a problem, but that ended when he was defeated for a second term by Reagan. Carter *wasn't a problem for what he knew but for what he wanted to know. He claimed to have seen a UFO in Georgia. He was egged on by Walter Jansen (more about him later). Carter peppered NASA, the FBI, the CIA, and the NSA with requests for information on UFOs. They fed him official looking gobbledygook in the hope that he would give up, which the voters finally forced him to do.*

One thing that's unclear to me is why only two presidents other than Truman knew of The Seven. Did the two discover The Seven by accident? Or did the members of The Seven think Kennedy and Reagan might be receptive to working with them? If that's the case, they were sure wrong about Kennedy. I'm not sure what Reagan thought.

But that's all history, before my time with The Seven. The current occupant of the Oval Office knows nothing of The Seven. And, to my knowledge, has zero interest in UFOs and aliens.

I know you hate me, but I liked you. I admired you for refusing to work for The Seven. It cost you. You lost Morgen. But maybe not forever.

The thought of Morgen caused Bill to stop reading. What the hell did West mean by "maybe not forever"? He quickly scanned the next paragraph, but there was no further mention of her there. Maybe later. He kept reading.

When I started working for The Seven, I was a true believer. I believed that the group's original mission, when it was created by Truman, was a noble one: protect the social and economic order. What I came to realize was that by the time I joined, that original mission had long been corrupted. What did you call The Seven? Murder Inc.? Not a bad description. The Seven had become a monster. It has killed hundreds, maybe thousands, of people in order to maintain its secrecy and power. It has violated every law on the books. In a way, it has become what it originally was created to prevent: a broken, lawless society.

Good soldier that I am, I never raised any objections to my increasing horrific work. But my refusal to object or expose The Seven was more than good soldiering. It was also fear. Once I was inside the tent, I would have simply been killed if I had stepped out of line. I saw it happen to others. It was with some effort that I kept it from happening to you. The initial plan was to offer you the opportunity to work for us, then kill you if you refused. But I was able to convince my superiors that the file I showed you would achieve the same results as killing you without any risk. After all, you're pretty high profile.

Bill, you'd be amazed at how big The Seven has become over the years. It has the blackest of black budgets, buried within budgets of the CIA and the NSA, plus military intelligence budgets. It also gets a ton of money from foreign countries that it has secret alliances with. Alliances not approved by the White House or the Senate, I might add. Thousands of people, both in and out of the military and the government, work for The Seven. Like any good secret group, it is highly compartmentalized. Only the top seven—What should I call them? The board of directors? Only they and their top aides have a complete picture of The Seven's operations. I don't know who they are. My rank in the organization was high enough to be in on the juicy rumors but not high enough to see the whole picture. And keep in mind, this is a group that is self-perpetuating. When one dies, the other six select his or her successor. All quietly done without the knowledge of the President or Congress. The Seven has even managed to convince just about everyone who has seen it that the original, and secret, document signed by Truman to create the group is fake, like the Majestic 12 papers that supposedly created another secret group. Anyone who suggests otherwise is quickly labeled a UFO kook. Perfect cover!

One other thing. Right before I had to be hospitalized, I heard reliable rumors that The Seven wanted to reduce the numbers in its ranks. The directors, or whatever they call themselves, apparently think the group's secrecy is threatened by its size. They may be right. They'll force people to quit and be silent by their usual methods: blackmail and murder.

I'm not sure what the ultimate goal of The Seven is anymore. They operate almost like a secret government. Will they eventually try to take over the government? Stage a coup? I think that's a real possibility, which is why I'm writing this letter to you. I do know this: The Seven has become a greater threat to our social order than if the government were to disclose that UFOs and aliens are real and that it has no idea why they're here or what they're up to.

You, Bill Sanders, must expose and stop The Seven. I know, I know. The file. But there are ways around that. You must work secretly in the beginning. Don't confront them head-on or expose them right away. Work from the outer edges toward the center. Gather as many powerful allies as you can. Especially contact those people who may have suspicions that something like The Seven exists. Talk to Walter Jansen. (Better hurry. Jansen's old as dirt now, but I think he still hobbles into his office at the Carter Center a couple of times a week. Pardon my gallows humor. It's the only kind I have left.) Remember, Jimmy Carter promised to release all government UFO files if he became President. When he was sworn in, he soon clammed up and never said another word about UFOs. Did somebody get to him? Or were his efforts thwarted by an unseen force he didn't realize was The Seven? Walter Jansen should know. Or at least be able to point you in the right direction. Warren Holden was smart to advise you to talk to Jansen, who has had an interest in UFOs ever since he saw one with Carter in 1969. In case you're getting a little paranoid, relax. Jansen is not involved with The Seven and knows nothing of it, although he may have vague suspicions. Maybe he has some secret UFO files from his White House years. Holden may have been on the verge of making some kind of move against The Seven when he had a heart attack in Santa Fe. After all, he knew about me. Do you know his wife? Talk to her. Maybe she'll let you see his files.

Work discreetly and gather your forces. It's been almost a year since we first met, and I showed you that file. The fact that you've been quiet since then puts you very low on The Seven's radar. They think you acquiesced to their threat and chose silence and inaction. They're not really paying attention to you anymore. I'm pretty sure of this because, believe me, I know how the police-military-bureaucratic mind works. At some point that file will become meaningless because you will have powerful people on your side who will deflect it. That's when you can make your move.

A warning: Be careful who you talk to. The Seven is everywhere. They have infiltrated every part of the government. They are in Congress, both as members and as staff. They are in federal agencies. They are in the military (need more proof than me?). They are inside the White House staff without the President's knowledge. Warren Holden was looking into The Seven's congressional links when he died.

Still wondering if you want to get involved? Let me play my trump card. The attack on the Air France jet that killed your wife was not a terrorist attack. It was a Seven operation from start to finish. Oh, the poor guy who got the bomb on the plane believed he was working for a jihadist group and was headed to paradise and all those virgins. The jihadists that set him up were operatives for The Seven. Their target was a single passenger, a California congressman named James Hand-forth. He was the chairman of the House Intelligence Committee and was planning to hold public hearings to investigate The Seven. If they had simply assassinated Handforth, there would have been all kinds of investigations. This way was much better from The Seven's point of view. He died simply because he was in the wrong plane at the wrong time. No suspicions of anything. No blowback. Your wife, I believe her name was Jane, was simply what we in the military call collateral damage. As were the other passengers.

Bill was stunned. He put the letter down. There were more than two hundred people on that flight. Collateral damage? The Seven killed Jane! He put his head down into his arms on his desk. He felt numb. Was West lying to him just to stoke his anger at The Seven? His gut instinct was that the colonel was telling the truth, knowing that death was near. If his gut was right, then The Seven really was out of control. But could a publicity-shy writer be the one to stop these monsters? He sat back up in his chair and glanced at the next paragraph. He saw Morgen's name and continued to read.

I know you're wondering about Morgen. When I told you that Morgen was working for The Seven and that you would never see her again unless you agreed to work for us, I had a feeling you would turn us down. I made her appear more negative than she is to help you let go of her. I have no way of knowing if it worked, but I can tell you now that Morgen is not an adventure junkie who loves money. She loves you, but she realized you two could never be together as long as The Seven existed and you wouldn't agree to work for them. She knew if she tried to quit, they would kill her. She did not betray you. She actually saved you by convincing me to blackmail you with the bogus file instead of killing you. I think she is as confused as the rest of us and has lost all faith in The Seven. She went to work for them for the same reason I did. She believed there was merit in their initial goal. She was smarter than me. She realized much quicker than I did that there was something rotten in what The Seven had become. We never talked directly about this. I am guessing—rightly, I believe—from things she hinted at or implied.

I have sent her a letter similar to this one, urging her to help bring down The Seven, but in the same careful way that I suggested to you. I don't know where she is. The night of our meeting she was flown to Rome. After that her whereabouts was outside of my bailiwick. So how did I send her a letter if I don't know where she is? I believe that the person I trusted to deliver the letter to her will find her. If he can't, he is to give her letter to you. If you don't have it by now, you can assume she does. In the letter I urged her to join forces with you. A matchmaker from six feet under. More gallows humor. Forgive me.

Well, Bill, as they say in the hackneyed world of politics, the ball is in your court. Do you want to play?

Regards and good luck.

Oddly, Colonel West didn't sign the letter. But Bill remembered his handwriting well enough to know the letter was authentic.

Bill put the taped envelope through a paper shredder next to his desk. The letter itself he neatly folded. He then stood up and took a few steps to one of his bookcases. He stuck the letter inside a copy of William Shirer's *The Rise and Fall of the Third Reich*. He thought Colonel West might have appreciated that.

He sat back down at his desk.

Do I want to play? I want to find Morgen and run away. But to where? And I have no way to find Morgen. I have to wait for her to contact me, if she ever does. The Seven bastards killed Jane. And my best friend. It's personal. I want to see them crushed. But how? Follow the advice of a dead man? If The Seven are allowed to continue, they will destroy this country as we know it, and probably some others along with it. Morgen and I will never be free as long as those fuckers exist. Play? This is not a game, West. This is a fucking war. A secret war. But a war, nonetheless, and I am an ill-equipped soldier. But fighting and winning it is the only way I get Morgen back.

CHAPTER 9

"I have some news you're not going to like."

Nancy Luke looked up from her salad and gave Bill a quizzical look. They were having their monthly Wednesday lunch at Dave's. It was almost a year ago to the day that Bill had announced to Nancy that he was going to Jefferson to help a friend.

"What's that?"

"I need to delay writing the Mideast book for a while. Maybe a month. Maybe two."

"My God, why?"

"It's personal. It involves events in Jefferson. It involves the death of my friend, Paul Watson, and the disappearance of his daughter. Some of that is still unresolved. I can't settle down to work with it hanging over my head. I can't tell you more now, but I promise you'll know everything at some point. I also promise that I'll deliver the manuscript of the Mideast book on time if we request the six-month extension. Nancy, you know me well enough to know that I will deliver."

"Yes, I do. But I worry about you. You seem obsessed by this Indiana business. At first you didn't want to go back out there to meet Jack Turner. Then as soon as English-Frostmann announced that Jack would be filming *Look Down* in Jefferson, you left the country to finish the research for the Mideast book. I had to fend off dozens of reporters who wanted to interview you. Now you want to take time off from a very profitable book project for maybe two months to chase whatever it is you're chasing. I haven't pressed you to tell me more than you wanted, but I sure am anxious to know what the hell is going on with my top-earning author."

"I understand. And you will know. I just need some more time. And for you to trust me. I will likely be out of town for the next few days, maybe a week or so. But I'll stay in touch."

Nancy reached across the table and put her hand on Bill's.

"Bill, you know I trust you and will support you whatever you do. Just keep me in the loop when you can."

Bill nodded.

Gerald, their usual waiter at Dave's, arrived with their main courses. They began to eat in silence.

Bill returned to his apartment after lunch and began to search through some files for Walter Jansen's cell phone number. He found it in the third file he opened. He remembered he had canceled a meeting with Jansen in Atlanta when The Seven's truck fires on the bridge to Louisville caused him to miss his flight. He canceled a second meeting when he fled Jefferson after he heard that Warren Holden was dead. He hoped Jansen would give him a third chance.

He dialed the number from his desk phone.

"Hello."

"Mr. Jansen?"

"Yes."

"Mr. Jansen, this is Bill Sanders in New York. We talked last year when I set up a meeting with you in Atlanta and then had to cancel twice, for which I apologize."

"I remember. You're the writer. You wrote that great book. *Points South*, I think was the title. Jimmy greatly admired it. I see in the papers that you've also written a best-selling novel that's going to be made into a movie. I don't read fiction. I also read that you're writing a book about the Middle East. I'll read that. When you called last spring, you were somewhat secretive. Said you didn't want to discuss anything on the phone."

"Yes, and that's still the case. Is it possible we could meet for an hour or so if I fly down to Atlanta?"

"Well, I'm ninety-two. I'm a little gimpy from arthritis, but I have most of my marbles. I still come to my office once or twice a week. In fact, I plan to come in tomorrow for a couple of hours. How about tomorrow afternoon at two?"

"That would be perfect. I'll fly down tonight or in the morning, depending on flights."

"Once you get here, ask somebody at one of the airport information desks for directions to the Carter Center. My assistant, Ruth Simpson, finally retired about six months ago. They didn't replace her because I'm here so little now."

"I remember her. We talked when I made my first appointment with you last year."

"Okay, Bill. See you tomorrow."

"Thank you, Sir. Goodbye."

"Bye."

After his call to Walter Jansen, Bill turned to his computer and clicked into his electronic address book. First, he entered Walter Jansen's cell number. Then he found Warren Holden's home number. He vaguely remembered that Warren's wife was named Betty. He had met her at a couple of cocktail parties in Washington several years ago. When he opened Holden's address file, there was her name: Betty. She was listed in the note category below the addresses and phone numbers for their home and his office.

Bill called the home number in Santa Fe.

"Hello."

"Is this Betty Holden?"

"Yes. Who's calling?"

"Mrs. Holden, it's Bill Sanders. I was a friend of Warren's. I'm a writer. I think we met at a couple of D.C. parties a few years ago."

"Oh, yes."

"I was devastated to hear of Warren's passing. He was very

helpful to me in many ways. I am so sorry for your loss."

"That's very kind of you. It took me a long time to finally realize he was gone. I still miss him terribly. I guess I always will. He often spoke of you. In fact, I just finished reading your novel, *Look Down*. I can't wait to see the movie."

"Did you know he had heart trouble, Mrs. Holden?"

"No. He never said a word about it. He wasn't a smoker and he wasn't overweight. He had an annual physical a few weeks before the heart attack. He was fine. I talked to his doctor and he said Warren had no symptoms of heart disease. But he also said that sometimes people with no symptoms have heart attacks. And please call me Betty."

"Thank you. The reason I called is I'm doing some research on the Middle East and on some events that took place around the time of Warren's death. He knew of them and was helping me when he died. I wonder if I might come out to Santa Fe and look through some of his files to see if he had found out anything between the time we talked and the time he died."

"You're welcome to come out, but there are no files to look at. I guess you didn't hear about the robbery or the murder?"

"No. What?"

"About a week after Warren's funeral, I decided to visit my sister in Silver City for a few days. Our cleaning lady, Rosa, agreed to spend nights at our house to take care of the dog while I was gone. The day before I was to return home, two men in a van with the name of a moving company printed on the side parked in front of the house. I don't know how, but they let themselves and a hand truck one of them was pushing in through the front door without breaking anything. They must have had a key or were very good lockpickers. Or maybe Rosa left the door open. It was a little after noon. She wasn't supposed to be there, but she had been working at another house in the neighborhood and told the owner, Rita Jones, that she wanted to check on our dog because he had been a little sick the night before. Jim Ross, a neighbor across the street, was working in his yard. He saw Rosa let herself into the house and then a few minutes later noticed the van and saw the men, who were wearing moving company uniforms, enter the house. He assumed it was something I had arranged with Rosa and didn't think much about them. He soon went inside to answer his telephone. He later told the police that he heard no sounds coming from our house. Rosa had apparently put the dog in the back yard as soon as she arrived. Police think the men first overpowered Rosa and gagged her with some rags; then they tied her up on the kitchen floor and shot her in the head. The police think the gun was equipped with a silencer because no one heard a shot. Then they went into Warren's office and loaded his two very full and very heavy file cabinets onto the hand truck, went back out the front door, carefully locking it behind them, and loaded the cabinets onto the van and drove away. The whole thing apparently didn't take more than ten minutes. I don't know what was in the file cabinets except copies of our tax returns and credit card bills. Bill kept all his legal work and files at the office. Our accountant had copies of the tax returns, and I immediately had the numbers changed on our credit cards."

It was the fucking Seven. Those murderous bastards. Killing an innocent cleaning woman they didn't even know in cold blood! I hope they rot in hell. Not just the killers, but also the higher-ups who authorized the operation.

Betty paused to stifle a sob and then continued.

"Rita became concerned when Rosa didn't return after an hour. She walked over to my house, found it locked, and was even more worried. She walked across the street to Jim's house and asked him if he had seen Rosa. He said he saw her let herself in and told her about the movers. Rita told me later she just knew something was wrong. She called the police. When they got inside the house, they found Rosa's body in a pool of blood on the kitchen floor. It must have been horrible for Rita and Jim to see. The police think the men killed Rosa so she wouldn't be able to identify them. Why they took only two file cabinets when the house was full of expensive furniture and Southwestern art remains a mystery.

"When the police called me in Silver City, I was frantic. I drove home that night. Benny—that's our dog—and I stayed with Rita for a week while the house was cleaned and the kitchen floor was replaced, which I insisted on. I thought of selling the place but couldn't bring myself to do it. Warren designed it himself and loved it.

"Rosa worked for several other people in the neighborhood, and we were devastated by her murder. She had a daughter, Elena, in high school. We held a city-wide fundraiser for her. We raised almost fifty thousand dollars. She has since moved to Albuquerque where she lives with some relatives. She's going to use the money for college."

"Betty, that's terrible. I'm so sorry. I didn't know any of this."

"Well, it was all over the news out here. Maybe there was nothing in the New York papers or TV."

"If there was, I missed it. But I think I was in Brussels when Rosa was killed. That could explain why I missed the news, if there was any out here."

"What kind of files were you looking for?"

"I'm not exactly sure. Some stuff on current events in the Middle East. I'm working on a book about the region, and Warren was helping me by providing the names of people he knew who might be able to help. He was compiling a list when he died."

Keep it simple. Don't spook her. Nothing about murders or UFOs.

"Well, as I explained, his two big file cabinets are gone. But you're welcome to come out and take a look at whatever is here. I know he had some boxes in the attic, but I don't know what's in them."

Worth a shot. Warren probably knew enough about The Seven to take precautions. Maybe he hid some files or other information in his attic.

"I have to be in Atlanta tomorrow. I'll try to book a flight from there to Albuquerque on Friday and drive up to Santa Fe late Saturday morning. Would that work for you?

"Yes, I think so. I'm getting my hair cut Saturday morning at nine, but I'll be home by ten."

"I'll probably arrive around eleven, but I'll call you first."

"Do you know where we live?"

"No, but I have your address, and I'll get a map and directions at the hotel in Albuquerque. I've been to Santa Fe several times, so I'm somewhat familiar with the city."

Maybe I'll get a GPS with the rental car. If someone will show me how to use it.

"All right, Mr. Sanders. I'll see you Saturday."

"Please, call me Bill."

"Okay, Bill. I'm looking forward to seeing you again. Warren always spoke highly of you."

"Thanks. Goodbye."

"Goodbye."

Bill booked a flight to Atlanta for nine-forty-five the next morning. He arranged another flight from Atlanta to Albuquerque for Friday. He booked a Hertz rental car for one day in Atlanta and another for three days in Albuquerque. He also arranged a room for one night at a Hilton Garden Inn in both cities and a room for two nights at the Inn of the Governors in Santa Fe.

Bill settled into a comfortable chair in Walter Jansen's office at the Carter Center. Jansen was a tall, thin man. Ramrod straight. He was nearly bald, his skin stretched tight against his skull. His eyes were gray and clear. He moved slowly and carefully as he closed his office door and walked to a chair next to Bill's. His voice was clear and strong, but with a flinty quality.

"My health is pretty good except for this damn arthritis. I just turned ninety-two last week. They say my mind is still good. Hope it stays that way. Now, what is it you have wanted to discuss with me for over a year that we couldn't do in a phone call?"

"Well, I'm aware that you were with President Carter in 1969—that was before he became governor of Georgia—when he said he saw a UFO. When he was running for President, he vowed to release all the information the government had on the subject. He not only didn't do that, but after he was sworn in, he never spoke of UFOs again."

"That's nothing we couldn't have talked about on the phone."

"True, but I'm not finished. I know from several sources that you were the one who pressured him to release the government's UFO files. I was told that after the 1969 sighting, you became passionately interested in the subject. But you kept quiet about it."

"Well, yes. Do you have any idea what an interest in UFOs can do to your reputation?"

"Of course. Which is part of the reason I didn't want to have this discussion on the phone. The government has big ears."

"Indeed, it does. What do you mean 'part of the reason'? What's the rest?"

"Mr. Jansen, I'm involved in a very strange series of events that started last year in Indiana when the ten-year-old daughter of my best friend vanished. My friend claims she was abducted by a UFO. He and two other people there were murdered; the girl has never been found. Jefferson, the town were all this took place, has been the location of a good many UFO sightings."

"What the hell does that have to do with me? Mr. Sanders, do you have something against being direct?"

"No, I don't. Is this direct enough? There is a dangerous, violent ultra-secret government organization that I believe is on the verge of staging a coup here and maybe in some other countries. Its leaders and members represent the greatest terrorist threat faced by the United States."

"What's that got to do with UFOs?"

"Hear me out. Without going into details of how, I have become aware of this group, known as The Seven, which has existed since after the Second World War and is manipulating public opinion so that people think the U.S. and other governments know more about UFOs and aliens than they let on and are in cahoots with them in exchange for advanced technology. They also work to make anyone who expresses a serious interest in UFOs to look like a lunatic. Right out of the X-Files. The Seven is covering up the fact that UFOs are real, and the government knows nothing about them. Nothing. The Seven fears that if the public knew UFOs were real, and the government has no knowledge or control of them, the social and economic order would break down. Plenty of studies have indicated that would be the case."

"I've heard about a secret document Truman was said to have signed dealing with UFOs. But word is that it's a fake."

"You're probably referring to the so-called Majestic 12 document. It is a fake. It was created by The Seven and then, in an operation orchestrated by them, was exposed as bogus. The whole episode cast a negative light on such groups and gave The Seven ever deeper cover."

"But a President would know about such a group. Jimmy would have known."

"No, not necessarily. The group is self-perpetuating, appointing its own members as they die or resign. It has the blackest of black budgets from the U.S. and even a few other countries. Other than Truman, only Kennedy and Reagan knew of The Seven."

"Even if this is true, why are you telling me?"

"Because, as I said, The Seven has become a threat to the country and to me. I need your help."

"Keep talking. Tell me more."

For the next hour, Bill told Walter Jansen almost all that had transpired since Paul Watson begged him to come to Indiana. He left out his affair with Morgen and the names of confidential sources; he didn't go into what he had discovered in Paul's notebook about his earlier abductions. He told Jansen about his meeting with Colonel West and about the letter from West that was delivered after his death. Bill also recounted what Betty Holden had told him about the robbery and murder at the Holden house shortly after the ex-senator's death.

"I've never heard of this Colonel West, but I remember reading something about that robbery and murder in a short story in The Washington Post last year. Senator Holden was a good man. We often discussed our mutual interest in the UFO phenomenon. He once held some hearings on them, but nothing came of it."

"Colonel West told me Warren was investigating The Seven when he died and saved them the trouble of killing him. I'm going to Santa Fe on Saturday to look through some boxes his wife says he kept in his attic."

"The existence of The Seven and the reality of aliens are all based on what one man told you? Do you know how crazy all this sounds?"

"I do. But the bodies keep piling up as a testament to the truth of it: my wife, Congressman Handforth, my friend, a young reporter, and a cleaning lady. And don't forget the two hundred or so people on the plane with Handforth and my wife. They and my wife were collateral damage, Colonel West said. And God knows how many others have been killed over the decades since the inception of The Seven."

Jansen didn't reply. He stared at a portrait of President Carter hanging above his desk.

Bill broke the silence.

"Mr. Jansen, can I ask you something?"

"I guess so."

"Why did President Carter go back on his promise to release all government files on UFOs? Why, once he was sworn in and NASA turned down his request to form a UFO study group, did he never speak of the subject publicly again?"

"Is this totally off the record? Just between us? Never to be spoken of or written about in any way?"

"Yes, if you wish."

"I wish. Jimmy didn't break his promise. During all four years of his presidency, he constantly pressured government agencies and departments, not to mention the military, to provide him with reports and files on UFO sightings. He wanted to know what the government knew, and he wanted to make it public.

"He was constantly stonewalled or given summaries that he knew weren't the whole story or that twisted the facts. The more he pushed, the more resistance he got. He once said to me that he thought some invisible force was working against him. He left the White House totally frustrated over two things: the hostages in Iran and his inability to get to the bottom of the UFO story. The public knew of the former frustration, not the latter. He considered discussing it with Reagan, but they didn't exactly get along—especially after Reagan's stunt with the hostages.

"So, the reason I've heard you out is I think what you call The Seven could have been that invisible force Jimmy encountered."

"Mr. Jansen, I need your help. Your guidance. The Seven must be stopped. But, as Colonel West pointed out in his letter, I ... we ... must be careful. We can't confront them head-on. They have the file I told you about that will make me look like a nut case. They could make us look like UFO crazies. They know how to do it. They could kill us. As I've made pretty clear, they know how to do that, too."

Walter Jansen didn't reply right away. He looked again at the portrait of Carter. He got up and walked stiffly to his desk. He opened a drawer and pulled out a piece of white paper, picked up a pen, and wrote several lines on it.

"I'm going to give you the name of a close, and I mean close, friend of mine who is a retired CIA agent. I can't emphasize enough how off the record and just between the two of us this is. He's twenty years younger than I am. You need to talk to him in person. His name is Jake McCoy, and he lives in Tucson."

Jansen walked from behind the desk and handed the paper to Bill.

"Here's his address and cell phone number."

"Why him?"

"Because like me, he's fascinated by UFOs. He tried a few times to see some files on them at Langley but was told they were restricted on a need-to-know basis. He also had a strong feeling that there were unseen forces that were thwarting his efforts. His experiences were similar to Jimmy's. Although he lacks the narrative and details of your experience, he is also convinced that there is a secret group working behind the scenes. Tell him what you've told me, and you'll have a powerful ally that you can trust one hundred percent. He can be your Virgil as you descend into this hell you've described.

"If you're going to Santa Fe, you'll easily be able to drive to Tucson and talk to him. I'll call and tell him you'll be in touch with him on, when, Sunday or Monday?"

"Probably Monday." *I have to remember to call Hertz and arrange to drop the car off in Tucson instead of Albuquerque.*

"I wish I were younger. I'd go with you."

CHAPTER 10

The Holden house was about a mile from the Santa Fe Plaza. It had taken Bill a little more than an hour to drive from Albuquerque to Santa Fe. It was too early to check in at the Inn of the Governors, but Bill left his bags there. The concierge gave him a city map and specific directions to the house. It was a stunning hacienda-styled adobe structure with a massive wooden front door. It was a little after eleven on Saturday morning when Bill rang the doorbell.

Almost immediately the door was opened by a short, attractive woman Bill instantly recognized.

"Bill Sanders?"

"Yes. It's a pleasure to see you again, although I know the circumstances bring back painful memories."

"Life has to go on. Please come in."

The house was spacious and beautifully decorated with Southwestern furniture and art. The tile floors were covered with Native American rugs.

"This is an amazing house. You said Warren designed it?"

"Yes. If he hadn't been a lawyer, he would have made a good architect."

Betty led Bill into the kitchen, where she offered him a seat at a round, wooden table inlaid with turquoise.

"Let's talk in here. Despite what happened to Rosa, it's still my favorite room. Does that sound weird or macabre?"

"No, not really."

"Would you like some coffee? I just made a pot."

"That would be great. Thanks."

"How do you like it?"

"Cream. No sugar."

Betty served the coffee, along with a plate of chocolate chip cookies.

The plate of cookies caught the attention of a medium-sized mixed-breed dog that had been sleeping in the kitchen.

"Can I give him a cookie?"

"Sure. You couldn't possible spoil him more than he already is."

"I'm surprised he didn't bark at me when I came to the door."

"He's hopelessly shy unless there are cookies involved. I'm sure he didn't bark when those awful people came in here and killed Rosa. She had put him in the back yard."

"Does he normally stay in the house?"

"Almost all the time. He only goes in the yard to do his business. Not long before he died, Warren built him a doghouse. Benny never used it, not even once. He continued to sleep every night right beside our bed like he has for the five years we've had him. I told Warren that Benny wouldn't use the doghouse, but he insisted on building it anyway. It's been in the backyard ever since. I think Warren just wanted a project."

"Sounds like it. How'd you pick the name Benny?"

"His real name is Bernard. Warren named him after an uncle he was fond of. I thought that was pretentious and started calling him Benny. Then so did Warren."

"Well, Benny's a nice dog."

Bill slipped him another cookie.

"So, Bill, tell me again what you're looking for."

"I'm not really sure. As I said on the phone, I'm working on a book about the Mideast. When Warren died, he was making a list of people he thought might be able to help me. I'm looking for that list plus anything else he came up with."

"Well, if what you're looking for was in either of those two big file cabinets, it's long gone. But there are those boxes I mentioned that he put in the attic. You're welcome to go through them. I think there are three."

Bill nodded and handed Benny another cookie.

✳

Betty led Bill upstairs to a hall closet in which there was a small inner door. She flipped a switch that turned on an over-head light. The closet was almost empty. Just some boxes and a couple of coats. She opened the inside door to expose a steep staircase to the attic. Betty flipped another switch that flooded the stairs and the attic with light.

"The boxes are at the top of the stairs to the right. I'll meet you down in the kitchen when you're finished. One flight of stairs is more than enough for my weak back."

"Okay. Thanks."

The cardboard boxes were right where Betty said they would be. The attic was almost empty. In addition to the boxes, there were a couple of small pieces of furniture covered with sheets.

The boxes, about eighteen inches in width and height, were not marked or labeled. The tops were loosely closed, not taped or sealed.

Bill opened the first box. It was full of handwritten letters, still inside their envelopes, from various people in various countries. The postmark dates covered at least twenty years. Bill read a couple of them. Just personal letters from friends. He put them back and closed the top flaps of the box.

The second box contained a manila envelope with Bill's name written on it in bold letters with a felt marker. There was nothing else inside the box. Whatever was inside the manila envelope was thick and heavy. Bill felt his stomach tighten as he opened the metal clasp. Inside was a file labeled "The Seven" that contained a thick sheaf of papers held to-gether with a big paper clip.

Bill sat on the stairs next to the boxes. He lay the manila envelope on the floor of the attic and turned to the third box. It was full of what looked like family photographs.

Envelope in hand, Bill walked down the attic stairs to the

closet on the second floor. He switched off the lights, closed the door to the attic stairs, stepped out into the hallway, and closed the closet door.

Betty was pouring a second cup of coffee when Bill walked into the kitchen. She offered him another cup, which he accepted.

She pointed to the envelope he was carrying.

"You must have found something."

"In the middle box. It was the only thing in there. Has my name on it. There's a file folder inside with some papers I haven't looked at yet."

Betty looked at Bill's name on the envelope.

"That's Warren's writing all right."

"The first box contained some personal letters; the third box was full of what I think are family pictures."

"I just have no idea when or why he put that stuff up there."

"Betty, can I photocopy the papers in this envelope?"

"You can have them as far as I'm concerned. I know Warren trusted you. He wrote your name on the envelope. He obviously meant those papers for you."

"Thanks. If you ever want them back, just let me know."

She nodded and refilled their coffee cups.

"Betty, I'm not leaving until tomorrow morning. Would you like to have dinner tonight? Is the restaurant at the La Fonda Hotel still as good as ever?"

"As far as I know, but I haven't been there in ages. That would be very nice."

"I'll make a reservation for, say, seven. How about if I pick you up at six-thirty?"

"I've got some errands to run later in the afternoon. Why don't we just meet at the restaurant at seven?"

"Sure. See you then."

✳

Back at the Inn of the Governors, Bill order a tuna salad sandwich and a glass of iced tea from room service. He made dinner reservations at the La Fonda for seven. He called Hertz and arranged to drop the car off in Tucson. Finally, he settled into a club chair and opened the envelope he had found in Warren's attic.

The paper clip held together twenty-three sheets of thick, white paper. Each page contained a handwritten label at the top followed by a handwritten list of names. The first sheet was labeled The Senate. Under that were the names of nine well-known senators, including Ross Duncan, the majority leader. There were five Republicans and four Democrats. The next sheet, labeled The House, contained a list of twenty-eight names. Bill recognized fewer than half of them. The third sheet—The White House—listed four names. Bill recognized two of them, including the press secretary, James Winston. The fourth sheet, labeled CIA, listed three names, including Robert Walker, the director. The remaining twenty sheets were for the Air Force, the Army, government agencies or departments, and two well-known Washington think tanks, the Brookings Institution and the Hoover Institution. Colonel Richard West was listed on the Army page. From the FBI and the NSA to the State Department, the Department of Agriculture, and the Department of Homeland Security, each labeled sheet contained a list of names. There was a sheet for the Secret Service with three names on it. Another list labeled The Washington Times had five names on it. Bill assumed they were reporters or editors, but he didn't recognize any of them. Another sheet labeled The Washington Post had two names on it. He didn't recognize them either. He wondered why for a few seconds, then realized that he had been out of the news business for more than a decade. A lot of people can come and go in ten years in a business as fluid as journalism.

These have to be names of people Warren believed were somehow connected to The Seven. But the lists by themselves don't mean much. Holden must have had some related documents, but where are they? If the lists are even half accurate and there are supporting documents, they could be a powerful weapon at some point. Maybe they would deflect the intimidating file Colonel West showed me. That CIA guy in Tucson that Jansen is sending me to will understand the lists better than I can. I hope.

Bill suddenly realized he had to protect these lists. Clearly, the men who took the file cabinets from Warren's house were looking for the lists and maybe more. Colonel West said in his letter that The Seven were going to kill Warren because he was threatening to expose them, and his heart attack saved them the trouble. Warren must have sensed the danger. Why else would have a put the lists in the attic?

Bill walked over to his bedside table, picked up the phone, and pressed zero for the front desk.

"Front desk. How may I help you, Mr. Sanders?"

"Is there a FedEx or UPS store near here where I can also photocopy something?"

"There sure is. A UPS store is less than two blocks away. I think they're open until six on Saturday, but we can make copies for you here in the office."

"Thanks, but I have quite a lot. Plus, I have to send it off, so I may as well do the copying there, too."

"I understand. Stop by the front desk on your way out and I'll show you on a map where the UPS store is."

"I will. Thanks."

Bill stuffed the lists back into the manila envelope and headed for the elevator and the lobby.

At the UPS store, Bill bought two manila envelopes. He made three copies of the lists and put one into each of the two envelopes, which he then sealed tightly with some thick, clear tape a clerk had given him. On the outside of one envelope he wrote: "George: Please keep this in a safe place for me until I return to New York. Also, please do not open it. Thanks, Bill Sanders." On the second envelope he wrote: "Max: Please stick this in one of your desk drawers until I contact you to pick it up. Please don't open. I'll explain when I contact you. Thanks, Bill Sanders."

Bill then had the first envelope sent to George Carson, the doorman at Eastside Towers in New York. The second went to Max Burris, an old friend and reporter at The Washington Post. Bill trusted Max, who had helped him reconnect with a source last year when he was looking for Colonel West.

Both envelopes were put inside larger, UPS packs. The clerk assured Bill that both packs would be delivered before noon on Monday.

Bill lay the third set of copies on top of the original and slipped both into the file folder marked "The Seven." Then he carefully put the folder back into the envelope with his name written on it.

Bill met Betty in the lobby of La Fonda. He had been so preoccupied earlier in the day at her house that he hadn't really noticed how beautiful and elegant she was. A petite brunette with soft features, he guessed she was in her early fifties, probably five or six years younger than Warren. She wore a cream-colored pants suit accented with a flame-red silk scarf.

"Hello, Bill. How nice of you to invite me to dinner."

"My pleasure. I've been eating too many meals alone lately."

"Me, too."

Betty smiled, and they walked across the tiled lobby to the colorful dining room where their table was waiting. After they were seated, both ordered margaritas.

"So, Bill, you've eaten here before, I gather?"

"Every time I come to Santa Fe, which isn't often enough. It's one of my favorite restaurants. They make guacamole from scratch right at your tableside. You can select the ingredients."

"I know. It's wonderful. But it's been several years since

I've eaten here. Warren didn't like to eat out. He always said eating out reminded him of lobbyists he hated but had to deal with in D.C."

"Shall we order the guacamole for a starter?"

"Absolutely."

After a waiter had prepared the guacamole to their liking in a large wooden bowl, they decided to enjoy it with a second margarita and wait a while before ordering dinner.

"You know, Bill, I think I owe you an apology."

"For what?"

"Well, today when you expressed condolences over Warren's death, I said nothing about your wife's death. Was it three years ago? I remember she was on a plane that was blown up by terrorists. That must have been horrible. I am sorry for both of us. I was touched that you dedicated *Look Down* to her memory."

"Thank you. It's been hard, although Jane's death has gotten easier for me to deal with in the last year. But if I think about it too much, all the pain comes back." *Especially because I know she was killed by The Seven, not the usual terrorists.*

"I understand, believe me. I try to stay busy."

Their waiter interrupted to ask if they were ready to order dinner. They decided they were and selected broiled salmon and a bottle of Santa Margherita Pinot Grigio.

"I'm pretty hungry, despite a sandwich I had for lunch after I left your house. And that guacamole."

"So am I."

The conversation turned to Santa Fe.

"I love living here. So did Warren. I don't think I could live on the East Coast again. I hated our years in D.C. Poor Warren not only didn't like living there, he was also constantly frustrated by all the political shenanigans. Do you like living in New York City?"

"I guess I've gotten used to it. It was a little overwhelming at first for an Indiana boy. It's a good base for a writer, but I have to admit that Santa Fe is pretty tempting. I love coming here."

When the waiter arrived with their dinners the conversation lagged as they turned their attention to the salmon.

As they were finishing dinner, Betty looked up at Bill.

"By the way, were those papers you found in the attic of any value to you?"

"I'm not sure. I looked at them this afternoon at the hotel, but I need to study them some more and try to cross-index them with some other stuff I have. Are you sure you don't want them back when I'm finished?"

"I'm sure. They're of no value to me. They were meant for you."

They decided to pass on dessert.

In the hotel lobby, Betty took Bill's hand.

"Would you like to come back to the house for some coffee and maybe an after-dinner drink?"

"Sure. I have to drive to Tucson tomorrow, but I don't have to be there until Monday, so I don't have to be on the road at the crack of dawn."

In the den next to the kitchen, Betty served fresh coffee and Grand Marnier. She had turned the gas fireplace on low, more for effect than heat. Betty sat next to Bill on a plush sofa. Benny was curled up on a carpet beside them.

"Can I ask you a personal favor?"

"Sure."

"Would you sleep with me tonight?"

Bill felt his neck getting hot and knew he was beginning to blush. He was speechless.

"Don't misunderstand. I'm not talking about sex. I'm not sure I'm ready for that yet. I simply mean would you sleep next to me in my bed and hold me?"

She began to cry.

"Now I've totally embarrassed myself. I hardly know you. But somehow, I trust you. You have no idea how lonely I am, especially at night. I hate sleeping alone."

"Me, too. But this is kind of sudden. It's been awkward for me since Jane's death. A year after she died, I had an affair with a teacher in New Jersey that didn't work out, and it was my fault. I had a brief affair with a younger woman last year, but that ended suddenly."

Betty wiped her eyes with a tissue.

"Bill, I'm not asking for an affair. I just want you to be with me and hold me for one night."

Bill reached out and touched Betty's cheek.

"I think spending a night next to each other might do us both good. Hope you have an extra toothbrush."

Betty smiled, stood up, and put Benny in his crate in the kitchen. She then led Bill upstairs to the master bedroom.

The next morning Bill was awakened by sunlight streaming through the bedroom window. He was on his right side with Betty's back tight against his chest. She stirred slightly as he kissed the back of her neck.

"I have to get going. Tucson awaits."

Betty turned over and faced him.

"Don't you want some breakfast first?"

"I'll get something to eat at the hotel after I shower and shave. You can stay in bed if you want. I'll put the dog out."

Betty took Bill's hand in hers.

"You have no idea what this meant to me. I haven't slept that well in months. Thank you."

"I slept pretty well myself, thank you."

CHAPTER 11

Bill arrived on the east side of Tucson a little after eleven on Monday morning. It was a hot day, and the traffic on I-10 was heavy. He had gotten started later than he expected on Sunday and had ended up stopping for the night at a roadside motel south of Truth or Consequences. But he had checked out early enough in Santa Fe to be able to cancel his second night's reservation at the hotel. He smiled as he was checking out and realized he had not slept even one night at the Inn of the Governors. When he left the room, the bed was turned down as the maid had left it Saturday night. There were a couple of chocolate mints still on the pillow.

Bill had called Jake McCoy before leaving Santa Fe and gotten directions to his house, which was easy to find. It was on the far east side of Tucson in an area of big homes on four- and five-acre lots. Most of the residents had small barns on their property where they kept horses. Many of the houses were adjacent to or near undeveloped state land that was crisscrossed with riding trails.

Jake McCoy's last name was on a mailbox at the end of a gravel road. A gate was open to a gravel driveway that wound around to his house, which was not visible from the road.

Bill pulled into the driveway and drove a few hundred feet to the house, which was a low and sprawling single-story structure made of adobe with an attached three-car garage. The front door opened, and a tall, muscular man dressed in blue jeans, cowboy boots, and a T-shirt stepped out and gave a wave. Bill got out of the car and headed toward him.

"You must be Bill Sanders. Welcome."

He stuck out his hand and Bill shook it.

"I am, indeed. You must be Mr. McCoy."

"Call me Jake."

"Only if you call me Bill.

"A done deal."

Jake had long black and gray hair pulled back into a pony-tail. He was tan, with sharp features and warm brown eyes. Walter Jansen had indicated Jake was seventy-two. He could pass for fifty-two, Bill thought.

"Bill, Walter tells me you have a complicated story to tell that I might be interested in. He says I should trust you. Should I? I haven't had a lot of experiences with writers. But I read *Points South* a couple of times. It's the real deal. And I trust Walter's judgment."

"Thanks. Yeah, I'm pretty sure I have a tale that will interest you. I also trust Walter Jansen. But I need to get to know you a little bit first. Let's talk and see if we like and trust each other."

"Fair enough. Come on inside. I made some chili for lunch. There's more than enough for two. I've also got some very cold Dos Equis Amber in the refrigerator, if you like Mexican beer."

"I do. Especially on a hot day."

The house was cool inside. They ate at a round oak table in a dining area next to the kitchen. Jake poured the Dos Equis into frosted mugs. In addition to the chili, there was hot cornbread and soft butter. A large window allowed a view of a swimming pool and another, smaller adobe house. All against a backdrop of the Rincon Mountains.

"This is great chili."

"Nothing special. No secret recipe."

"What an amazing house and view. When was it built?

"The main part was built in the early thirties. But it's been added on to since then. I built the pool and guest house about ten years ago. I don't ride or have horses, so I tore down an old barn to make room for the casita."

Bill finished his beer.

"Want another? I do."

"Sure."

Jake got fresh frosted mugs from the freezer and filled them with beer.

"So, Jake, tell me a bit about yourself. Then I'll introduce you to me."

"I'm a retired CIA field agent, which I think Walter told you. I grew up in a small town near Orlando, Florida. I majored in French in college and discovered that I had a knack for languages. I speak four fluently, five if you count English. When I graduated, I joined the Navy and was sent to the military's foreign language school in Monterey. After that I worked in Naval intelligence. After four years in the Navy, I was recruited by the CIA. I worked there for thirty years. Retired at fifty-six and been living out here ever since. Sixteen years. Longest I ever lived in one place."

"What did you do in the CIA?"

"I can't talk in detail about much of it, but the usual stuff. Mainly collecting intelligence. I worked some in Washington, a lot in Europe and South America. Some in the Middle East, a little in Asia. It was my experience in South America that enabled me to appreciate *Points South*. Walter tells me you're working on a new book about the Mideast."

"I've been researching it. I plan to start writing it soon. Should take eighteen months to finish."

"Well, if it's as good as *Points South*, it'll be a winner."

"Thanks. How did you get to know Walter Jansen?"

"I was assigned to the White House during the last year of the Carter Administration. Although Walter was twenty years older than me, we became good friends. Really good friends. We still are."

"Are you married?"

"I was. Once. For ten years. But my career was not exactly compatible with marriage. You?"

"I'm a widower. My wife was killed in an airplane crash three years ago."

"I'm sorry."

"Thanks. I'm still not over it, but I'm getting there. I'll tell you more about it later."

Jake stared out the window at the sunlight dancing on the surface of the pool.

"Tell me some more about yourself."

"I was born and raised in Jefferson, Indiana, a small town in the southern part of the state along the Ohio River. I graduated from Indiana University with a major in English literature and a minor in psychology. But all I was ever really interested in was journalism and writing. During my college years I worked summers for my hometown paper, The Jefferson Courier. My first big newspaper job after college was with The Louisville Courier-Journal. Then I moved to the Houston Chronicle and eventually to The New York Times where I worked in the Washington bureau. I left the Times about 10 years ago to write books. *Points South* was my breakthrough book. I have a novel out called *Look Down* that's going to be made into a movie. It'll be directed by Jack Turner."

"I'm impressed. Jack Turner's a big name in Hollywood. I read something about your novel in the paper, but I haven't read fiction in years."

"That's something you have in common with Walter Jansen."

Jake smiled.

"I told you we were close."

"Anyway, I went back to my hometown last year to help an old friend, whose ten-year-old daughter was missing. That was the beginning of what you called my complicated story."

"Let's cut to the chase. What brings you out here to see me?

"Didn't Jansen tell you?"

"Are we dancing around three letters we're both hesitant to say?"

"Maybe. Would they be UFO?"

"Bingo!"

"Jansen told me you were fascinated by the UFO phenomenon. Now I find out you worked in the Carter White House.

Did the CIA know of your interest in such stuff?"

"Let's back up. We can get into that later. First, tell me all about your trip to Jefferson to help your friend find his daughter. Explain to me how it became so 'complicated,' as you call it."

"Well, settle back, Jake. Maybe we should have another beer before I start."

"Good idea."

Jake got two more frosted mugs from the freezer and filled them with Dos Equis Amber.

Jake sat back down at the table.

"Now I think we're ready."

For the next hour or so, Bill told Jake McCoy essentially what he had told Walter Jansen about all that had transpired since he drove to Indiana to help Paul Watson, including his meeting with Colonel West. Only this time he did not leave out his relationship with Morgen. He also related what he had discovered in Paul's notebook about his friend's childhood abductions. He was more detailed in his description to Jake of the letter from Colonel West and the robbery and murder at Warren Holden's house shortly after the ex-senator's death. He also told Jake about the lists he found in Warren Holden's attic. The only things he left out were the names of confidential sources and the fact that he spent Saturday night in Betty Holden's bed.

Jake took a long sip of beer.

"What do you want from me?"

"I need your help. I want to expose The Seven before it's too late. These people have to be stopped. Whatever disruptions arise from the public knowing the truth about UFOs and the government pale by comparison to the danger posed by The Seven. I need the help of somebody I trust without question. I need somebody who knows his way around, who can tell the good guys from the bad guys. Walter Jansen said that would be you if I told you my story."

"Do you have the letter from West and Holden's lists?"

"Yes. The letter is in my apartment in New York. The lists

are in my backpack in the car. I should have brought the letter with me, but I didn't even know about you when I left it in my home office."

"I never heard of this Colonel West. Let me see the lists. I may have met Warren Holden a couple of times back in the day."

Bill nodded and went outside to his car. He returned with his backpack, which he placed on the table. He unzipped it and pulled out the envelope containing the original lists and the copy he made. He handed the copy to Jake.

"Is this your only copy?"

"No. I sent two copies to two different friends, one in New York and one in Washington, with instructions that they not open or read them. They are to simply hold them until I pick them up in person. I trust the two will do just that. Anyway, the lists don't really mean anything without context."

"Perhaps, but you can never tell. You've stepped through the looking glass. Things are not always what they seem. You were smart to mail those copies."

Jake took a pair of reading glasses from his shirt pocket, propped them on his nose, and spent the next few minutes studying the lists.

Finally, he looked up.

"I know, or know of, most of these people. I've been retired from the CIA for a long time, but I still keep up with stuff. I also still have a few good contacts with the Firm.

"A good many of these people Holden listed have anti-government sentiments. At least four of them are pushing secessionist movements in their home states. Almost all are in lock step with the NRA when it comes to guns. If you're right about all this, my guess is they see The Seven—or what it has become—as a route to stage a coup. I suspect few of them have much interest in UFOs. The problem is these lists by themselves don't prove anything. Holden must have had something else tying the people on these lists to The Seven."

"I agree. There must be some supporting documents. I can check again with Betty. Maybe there a safe deposit box or something. What else can we do?"

"We? I haven't agreed to help you or get involved."

"Will you?"

"Of course. If Walter vouches for you, you've got no problem with me. Plus, I've been bored shitless out here. And I've always been fascinated by UFOs. Every time I tried to bring up the subject at the CIA, I hit a roadblock. It always seemed as if somebody high up was pulling strings in the background to keep the subject confusing and amorphous. I also got not-so-subtle hints that interest in UFOs was not exactly career-enhancing. As a result, I mostly kept my interest in UFOs to myself. But when I got assigned to the White House and became friends with Walter, that changed. Carter was also pushing for information on UFO sighting and running into the same roadblocks I did earlier at the Firm. He was President, so his roadblocks were gentler and more sophisticated than mine were. But they were roadblocks, nevertheless. Walter and I were drawn to one another when we discovered our mutual interest in UFOs and aliens. It was through Walter that I learned of Carter's inability to get to the truth of UFOs and alien visitations. Now Walter sends me you and the pieces of the puzzle begin to fit together. It sounds like The Seven is the key to understanding all the confusion and ridicule that has surrounded UFO research and researchers. Plus, it sounds like The Seven have turned into the bad guys. Killing a ten-year-old girl makes you a bad guy in my book. It's always fun to fight the bad guys. But who the hell are The Seven? Are they government and military officials? Are they from the private sector? Or a mixture? Were Warren Holden's lists an effort to find these seven men or women? Or were the lists simply a roster of people who are foot soldiers for The Seven, like your Colonel West? Except for a couple of think tanks and a newspaper, the lists are of government types. Jesus, the CIA director and the Senate majority leader."

"I don't know the answers to any of those questions. I think the whole operation must be highly compartmentalized to have maintained such tight secrecy over the years. I'm not sure where West was in the hierarchy, but I'm pretty sure he didn't know the identities of those at the top of The Seven. If you could read his letter, I think you would agree that he would have included names if he knew them."

"Can I keep this copy of Holden's lists?"

"Sure."

"I also need to see that letter from West."

"Then you'll have to come to New York, or I'll have to come back out here."

"I'll come to New York. I need a change of scenery."

"Jake, we may be looking at some significant travel expenses in the next few weeks or months, depending on where all this takes us. I've made a lot of money over the past few years from my writing. Let me take care of these expenses."

"No need. I guess Walter didn't tell you. My father was a chemist. He invented a special kind of synthetic glue used in all kinds of manufacturing. He sold the patent rights to a big multinational for twenty million dollars. He died two years later. My mother died a year after he did. I was an only child. I have no children. I can afford to travel for a long time. End of story."

"If you say so."

"I say so."

"Well, I need to find a hotel room for a couple of nights. What if we fly to New York on Wednesday? I could use a day just to take it easy."

"You don't need a hotel room. Stay in my casita. That's what it's for. I recommend you fly to New York on Wednesday, and I'll follow later in the week. I'll call you when I get there. Maybe I'm a little paranoid, but old habits are hard to break. We don't want to arouse any suspicions. If this West character said you're flying below The Seven's radar, let's try to keep it that way.

"How about if I show you around Tucson tomorrow? Have you been here before?"

"Yes, but only briefly. I was here on a couple of presidential trips when I covered the White House. Had to work and didn't see a lot. A tour is a good idea. It would not only give me a break, but we could also get to know each other better."

"Good point. Do you like Mexican food?"

"Sure do."

"I know the place. Let's get you settled in the casita. Then later we'll have a drink, watch the sunset, and then head out for dinner."

"Sounds good."

Chapter 12

Bill arrived in New York late Wednesday afternoon, after a brief layover in Houston. As soon as he walked into the lobby of Eastside Towers, he asked George for the envelope containing a copy of the Holden lists. George walked over to his desk, pulled a key from his pocket and unlocked a bottom drawer where he had stashed the envelope. Bill took it and handed George a twenty-dollar bill.

"Thanks, Mr. Sanders. And welcome back."

"Thank you, George."

When Bill reached his apartment on the thirty-second floor, the first thing he did was pull Colonel West's letter from *The Rise and Fall of the Third Reich* and read it again. He read it one more time after a dinner of soup and cheese and some bread that was still relatively fresh. The next morning, he walked a block and a half to a FedEx store and made two copies of the letter. He then walked three more blocks to his bank, where he put one copy of Colonel West's letter and the unopened envelope he had mailed to George in his safety deposit box. The other copy of the letter he took back to his apartment, along with the original, which he refolded and stuck back in *The Rise and Fall of the Third Reich*. He slipped the copy into the middle drawer of his desk.

Bill picked up his desk phone and dialed Nancy Luke's office number. Linda, one of her assistants, answered.

"Hi, Linda. It's Bill Sanders. Is Nancy available?"

"For you, always. Hold on."

The background music on the phone was the theme from *Star Wars*.

"Bill, where are you?"

"Back in town. I got in late yesterday afternoon. I tried to call you then, but you had gone for the day. I didn't want to bother you at home."

"Are you making progress with whatever it is you working on?"

"I think so. But I need more time."

"Well, you said a month, maybe two. So, I'm expecting that. Are you going to be here or traveling?"

"Both, but I'm playing it by ear. I wanted to let you know that there are some gaps in what I'm doing so I think I'll be able to start writing on a sporadic basis until I get things resolved."

"That's great news. Type fast. This book is going to be big."

"I'll do my best."

"I know you will. You always do."

"Thanks. I appreciate that."

"By the way, I spoke to Jack Turner on Tuesday. They expect to name the actors for *Look Down* sometime in July. He said they had originally planned to start filming in late August, but they may move that up to the middle of August. Things must be going pretty smoothly."

"That's good news for us and Jefferson. I hope to get out there while they're filming, maybe in early September. You want to go with me?"

"Maybe. Let me think about it and look at my schedule."

"Okay, Nancy. Later.

"Bye."

Bill spent all day Friday and most of Saturday morning working on his Mideast Book, which he had tentatively titled *Power Points*. By early Saturday afternoon, he had heard nothing from Jake McCoy. He thought about sending him a text message but decided to wait a while longer. Just as he was about to return to his computer, his cell phone chirped. It was Jake.

"Hello, Jake. Welcome to New York."

"I just got here. I'm in an Uber car headed for the hotel."

"Why don't you stay at my apartment? You know you're welcome."

"Thanks. But I think it's best if we not be seen together so much, at least in New York or Washington. I'm staying at the St. Regis. Let me get settled in and I'll call you back. How about dinner tonight?"

"Absolutely."

"You pick the place and make a reservation. How about someplace that's quiet so we can talk?"

"Will do. I'll await your call."

"Deal."

Bill called Chez Maurice, a quiet little French restaurant he liked that was only a few blocks from the St. Regis. He made a reservation for seven and returned to his computer and *Power Points*.

An hour later his cell chirped again.

"So, where and what time is dinner?"

"Seven. At Chez Maurice, a French place not far from your hotel. I think they require a jacket."

"Good. I'll get directions from the concierge. See you there at seven."

Jake abruptly ended the call.

Bill hoped mentioning the jacket didn't offend Jake. In Tucson, he had worn nothing but blue jeans, cowboy boots, and a T-shirt.

Bill showered and dressed. He opened his middle desk drawer, took out the copy of the West letter, folded it into thirds, and slipped it into his inside jacket pocket. He took a taxi to the restaurant. Jake was already there, having a drink in the bar.

Bill hardly recognized him. He was wearing a blue blazer, a crisp white shirt, tan slacks, and expensive loafers. His ponytail was gone. His hair was neatly cut, barely reaching the tops of his ears. He looked even younger than he did in Tucson.

They shook hands. Bill ordered a martini, slightly dirty

with an olive.

"What's with the haircut?"

"This trip was an excuse to get rid of my long hair. This woman I've been seeing on and off—lately, mostly off—has been bugging me to get a regular haircut."

The maître d' interrupted to show them to their table.

Both ordered appetizers of steamed mussels in a white wine sauce and steak frites with béarnaise sauce for the main course. Bill selected a bottle of Bordeaux to go with their steaks.

"Did you go through Dallas or Houston to get here?"

"Neither one. I flew on the shuttle from D.C."

"What? When did you go to Washington? What were you doing there?"

"I flew to D.C. on Thursday from Phoenix to get a direct flight. I spent most of Friday meeting with some old friends of mine from the CIA. They wouldn't have talked to me on the phone. Any phone. Not anymore."

"I found that out last year when I was trying to find Colonel West."

"I wanted to dig into your story from some other angles. I needed to get a sense of what you were talking about from some other people who might know something without fully realizing it, if you get what I mean."

"You mean like a hunch something isn't right? Like the roadblocks you and President Carter ran into? Even if the person with the hunch isn't chasing UFOs or even concerned about them."

"Exactly."

"And?"

"The people I talked with pretty much confirmed your suspicions."

Their waiter interrupted to serve the mussels, steaming in a white wine broth. Both men paused their conversation to taste them.

"You mean that something is amiss?"

"Yeah. And listen, when the Deep State thinks there is

some deeper force at work, I pay attention."

"Do they see The Seven, this force, as a threat? Like a coup or something that Colonel West wrote about in his letter?"

"I'm not sure yet. By the way, I need to see that letter."

"I have a copy for you in my jacket pocket. Let's walk back to your hotel room after dinner, and you can read it there."

"Sounds like a plan."

✳

Jake's room at the St. Regis was, in fact, a suite.

"I guess you weren't kidding when you said you had plenty of money."

"Nope. And I don't travel much these days. When I do, I go first class."

Both men were sitting in wing-back chairs in the suite's living room. Jake had ordered a bottle of brandy from room service, which he opened and poured generous portions into two snifter glasses on a marble coffee table.

"Now can I see the letter?"

Bill nodded and reached inside his jacket pocket and handed the folded pages to Jake, who was adjusting his reading glasses.

Bill sipped his brandy in silence for the next few minutes as Jake slowly read the West letter.

"What's the deal with Morgen? According to West, she must have gotten the letter. But you haven't heard from her, right?"

"No, I haven't. I don't know how to contact her or even look for her. All I can do is wait for her to contact me, if she does. Maybe The Seven are suspicious of her. Maybe she's under surveillance. Maybe she can't contact me without putting herself in danger. I hope West wasn't jerking me around about her. But why would he?"

"I don't think he was."

"What's our next move?"

"I need to go back to D.C. for a few days. Talk to some

more people, especially about the Holden lists."

"You can keep that copy of the letter."

Jake shook his head and handed it back to Bill.

"No, you keep it. The Holden lists are anonymous. Having the letter would link me to you."

"Whatever you think works. You're the expert."

The two had a second snifter of brandy.

"Jake, could this be as big a deal as it seems? Could there really be a secret group ... I mean really secret but big enough and powerful enough to threaten the government or seize power? When I was a reporter it always seemed to me that secrets were hard to keep for long, especially in Washington."

"Depends on the secret and who's keeping it. The Seven seems to have done a pretty good job by using misinformation and ridicule, along with some serious compartmentalization. As to being big and powerful enough to stage a coup, maybe. Our so-called democracy is actually pretty fragile. It doesn't take much to shake things up. Getting people really scared helps. Remember, in the wake of 9/11 Congress approved legislation that allowed the government to secretly lock anybody up indefinitely without giving a reason. So long, habeas corpus. People accepted it without a whimper. Maybe The Seven plans something like that. What bothers me a bit is that much of what we are chasing is based on what this Colonel West told you in your meeting and in the letter I just read. Sure, we have the indirect evidence of unseen forces at work. Like the kind that I think thwarted Carter and me, as well as others. But it's only West who warns of a coup. Do we believe him? Do we believe him that UFOs are real? Does it actually make any difference? Doesn't The Seven still need to be taken down? After all, your experience has shown that The Seven is not a collection of nice guys. Too many dead bodies for that. Would they go to such lengths just to protect a UFO secret? Or are they doing such things to protect themselves from public exposure while they plan a takeover? This is what I need to get settled in my own mind, and why I need to go back to D.C. for a few more days."

"When will you go?"

"Tomorrow morning. I'll be at the Mayflower Hotel. It's Spook Central."

"While you're gone, I'll be working on my book. But I can stop anytime. Call when you're ready to come back here or want me to come down there."

Chapter 13

Bill was working at his computer when his cell phone rang with a pleasing trill. *I'm glad I finally got on Google and figured out how to change that ring tone.*

"Hello."

"Bill, it's Betty Holden."

"Hi, Betty. What a pleasure to hear from you. What's up?"

"Something terrible has happened."

"What?"

"I came back to Santa Fe yesterday after spending a few days with my sister in Silver City and discovered my house had been ransacked. I mean really ransacked. Whoever did it was looking for something. Every drawer, every closet was opened, and the contents dumped on the floor. Paintings were pulled off the wall. All the food in the refrigerator and freezer was dumped on the kitchen floor. Dishes were broken. Mattresses were pulled off the beds. Those boxes you looked at in the attic were carried to the second floor and their contents dumped in my bedroom. They got into Warren's tool bench in the garage and scattered his tools everywhere. They even broke into his car and cut open the seats and forced the trunk open. So far as I can tell, nothing is missing. What could they have been looking for? Surely not those papers you found in a box in the attic and took? Were they the same people who killed Rosa last year and took the file cabinets? It must have happened at night because nobody in the neighborhood saw anything. Why would anybody do such a thing. What were they looking for?"

"I don't know, but I doubt it was those papers I took. They

were just lists of people who Warren thought might be able to help me with my research."

"Thank goodness I had the dog with me. None of the locks were damaged. The police said whoever got in had a key or was able to pick a lock."

Betty began to cry.

"Do you want me to come out there and help you? What about your sister? Can she come up from Silver City?"

"No. Her husband isn't well, and she needs to take care of him. And I don't want to impose on you. I know you're in the middle of a book project. Besides, I have friends here who are helping me."

She sniffed and continued in a stronger voice.

"I've decided to sell this house as soon as I get it put back together and repaired and cleaned. I can't live here anymore. In fact, Benny and I are staying with Rita Jones, a neighbor, right now. This on top of Warren's death and Rosa's murder is too much. I'm going to move to Silver City to be nearer to my sister."

"Betty, that might be a wise move. I'm so sorry this happened. And I will come out if you want me to."

"I appreciate that, but I'll be fine."

"Are you calling me on your cell phone?"

"Yes. Why?"

"I just wanted to be sure I have your cell number in case I need to reach you. Call me if you need anything."

"Thanks. I will. Bye."

"Bye."

The Seven again. This is getting insane. Those guys must have been looking for the lists I found in Betty's attic. But why the long wait between the first break-in when they killed the cleaning lady and took the file cabinets? Did my visit to Betty trigger this? Are they watching her house? Or me? Or both of us? Is my phone tapped? If they were looking for the lists, they obviously didn't know I had taken them. They must have thought they were still in the house somewhere. Or were they looking for something else entirely? Documents that explain the lists? This is not making any sense.

✳

Bill called Jake McCoy's cell.

"What's up Bill?"

"We need to talk. But not over the phone."

"Understood. Why don't you come on down? Call or text me when you get here."

"Okay."

Bill took the Acela from Penn Station to Union Station in Washington. During the trip, he read the lists over two more times. He had stuck the copy of Colonel West's letter into a deep compartment of his backpack but didn't read it again. It was after four o'clock when he finally got a taxi to the Hay-Adams Hotel, where he had made a reservation. When he was settled into his room, he sent a text to Jake. Two words: "I'm here."

Within seconds, he got an answer: "Vietnam Memorial. 6 p.m."

✳

The tourist crowds had thinned out when Bill arrived at the memorial. At first, he didn't see Jake. Then he felt a tap on his shoulder.

"Hi, stranger."

Bill turned around and they shook hands.

"That was quick."

"I took the Acela. Almost as fast as flying when you take into account travel time to and from airports."

"Let's take a walk and talk."

Jake led the way across the mall toward the Reflecting Pool.

When they were out of earshot of anyone, Jake looked at Bill.

"So, let's talk."

Bill recounted the ransacking of Betty Holden's house.

"It had to be The Seven and they had to be after those

lists. Betty said nothing was missing. But why did they wait so long after taking the file cabinets? Or were they looking for something else? Other incriminating documents? Was it because they were somehow keeping track of me? But why would they assume my visit meant anything or that I was taking anything out of the house? If they thought I took something, why would they ransack the house? Why wouldn't they come after me? Nothing seems to make any sense."

"I agree. It is confusing. Maybe it'll make sense as we move along."

"Did you learn anything at Spook Central?"

"Yes. Maybe. I feel like I'm grasping at shadows. But I've spoken to several old hands I trust at the agency. Unlike a lot of the new guys, they have an institutional memory and a sixth sense for picking up on a lot of things other people in the business might miss. All of them seemed almost relieved when I started asking questions about things not feeling right, being out of kilter. They've been feeling the same way but were afraid to talk to anyone. Such talk could be very career-limiting. But they've known me for decades and they trust me and know I'm no threat."

"What are they picking up?"

"That something big is in the works. They don't know what it is or where it's coming from. You know how animals can sense an earthquake before it strikes? It's the same kind of thing. A feeling. A feeling about the way certain people act or talk. A sense certain people are lying, that things are being concealed. But by whom? For what reason? I'm beginning to think we should believe Colonel West's letter."

"Jake, should we go back to Atlanta and talk to Walter Jansen again? Remember, West suggested in his letter that Jansen might have some secret UFO files. And when I talked to Warren Holden just before he died, he mentioned the possibility of a secret cache of UFO files at the Carter Center. I should have brought this up with Jansen when I was in Atlanta. I guess I got sidetracked filling him in on what happened in Indiana and later in my meeting with West."

"Maybe. But first I want to go over those lists from Holden again. Carefully. Name by name. I recognized many of them, but some I didn't. We need to find what we can about each one. Do you have a laptop with you?"

"Yes. In my hotel room."

"Let's go separately. I'll meet you in the lobby in forty-five minutes."

"Sure. Okay."

*

When Jake showed up in the lobby of the Hay-Adams, he was carrying a plastic shopping bag.

"I stopped at a drugstore and bought some three-by-five cards. They help me think. We can put each name on a card, along with key information."

In Bill's room, they wrote each name onto a card and organized the cards the same way the lists were organized. There were nine cards for members of the Senate and twenty-eight cards for members of the House of Representatives. There was a total of seventy-eight names. The other forty-one were sorted according to the organizations with which Warren Holden had listed them. Bill and Jake could identify all but twenty-two of the total number.

In less than an hour at Bill's laptop, they had found twenty-one of the unknowns. Eleven of those were congressmen, mostly from rural districts. The only name they couldn't find was a member of the House named Bernard T. Perro.

Jake was puzzled.

"Something's wrong. All the other names on Holden's lists check out. Why would he include on his House list someone who's not a congressman?"

"Wait a minute! Isn't "perro" the Spanish word for dog?"

"Yes. So What?"

Without saying another word, Bill grabbed his cell phone, looked up Betty Holden's cell number, and called it.

"Hello."

"Betty, it's Bill Sanders. I'm in D.C. Are you still staying with your neighbor?"

"Yes. Rita Jones."

"Have you put your house on the market yet?"

"Not yet. It's still being cleaned and repaired. Maybe next week. Why?"

"Betty, is the doghouse Warren built still in the back yard?"

"Yes. It's about the only thing that wasn't torn apart when they ransacked the house."

"Listen, Betty. I'll explain later, but I need to see that doghouse. Don't let anyone touch it or haul it away. Just trust me. I'll try to fly out there tomorrow with a friend. We should be there by late afternoon. I'll call you from the airport and you can meet me at your house. Is that okay?"

"I suppose. What's this all about, Bill?"

"I'll explain when I get there. Is it all right if I bring a friend? He knew Warren and is helping me."

"Sure. Okay, I guess. So, I'll see you tomorrow?"

"Unless I can't get a flight, in which case I'll call you."

"Well, bye for now."

"Bye, Betty."

Jake was looking even more puzzled.

"What the hell was that all about?"

"Their dog's name is Bernard. They call him Benny. Bernard T. Perro. Bernard The Dog."

"So? Was Warren just making a joke?"

"I don't think so. Betty told me that not long before he died, Warren insisted on building a doghouse for Benny, although the dog never used it. He sleeps beside their bed. Betty said Warren must have wanted a project. I think Warren built that doghouse to hide something and left a clue in his House list.

"Jesus. As weird as that sounds, you may be right. Glad you told Betty I'm coming, because I will."

"If we can get a flight."

"Don't worry about that. Let me spend some of my father's money before I die. We'll charter a business jet."

"Why don't we split the cost?"

"No way. But you can buy me dinner tonight. How late is the restaurant in this joint open? I could sure use a drink and a steak."

✳

Bill and Jake met for an early breakfast the next morning at Bill's hotel.

"I called last night. We're all set with the plane. It leaves from Reagan National at 10:30."

Bill nodded, took a sip of coffee, and glanced down at a copy of The Washington Post that had been delivered to his room. The top stories were the usual blend of national and international news. There was a picture of the President walking across the south lawn of the White House toward Marine One. Bill unfolded the paper and glanced at the articles below the fold.

"Holy shit! Did you see this?"

"What?"

Bill pointed to a two-column headline:

Former Top Aide to Carter
Killed by Hit-and-Run Driver

Bill read the top of the story aloud, skipping the Atlanta dateline.

"Walter Jansen, a former assistant to President Jimmy Carter, was killed last night in front of his home by a hit-and-run driver.

"Police said Jansen, 92, was pronounced dead at the scene on Grayson Avenue in the upscale Buckhead section of the city.

"Investigators said Jansen, a widower who lived alone, was starting to take a walk around 7 p.m. when a red Ford Mustang swerved off the roadway, drove up on the sidewalk and struck Jansen from the rear. At least two neighbors witnessed the incident.

"Jansen, a member of the board of the Carter Center, had reported a break-in at his home earlier in the day. He told police someone broke in through the back door while he was working at the Carter Center between noon and 2 p.m. He said the only things that appeared to be missing were some personal files from his home office.

"The red Mustang, which was brand new, was found abandoned less than a mile away. It had been reported stolen from a local Ford dealership the night before. Police speculate that the driver was picked up by an accomplice when he abandoned the car. Investigators said they had no leads but were questioning residents in the area where the Mustang was found. Police said they were treating the case as a homicide.

"Jansen was a top national security adviser to President Carter ...."

Jake was ashen.

"That wonderful old man. I loved him. Who the fuck would do such a thing?"

Bill flushed, fighting back tears.

"I'll tell you who. The fucking Seven, that's who. That's the same crap they pulled when they blocked me from crossing the bridge in Louisville. Steal new vehicles, abandon them, and flee in a getaway car. I bet the police later find the second car abandoned somewhere. And you know they're the same people who broke into Jansen's house earlier and took the files. They'll never catch who did this."

"But why would they kill Jansen now? Was he a threat? Maybe he did have some files like Holden suggested, but what were they? Were they the lists that we have? Does this mean they have no idea we have them, too? Why did they wait a year to go after them again? West said he stopped them from killing you because you were high-profile. So was Jansen. A former top White House aide, for Christ's sake."

"I don't know. This isn't making sense."

"So, what do we do now?"

"Stick with our plans, I guess. We can't help Jansen. Does he have relatives?"

"Yes, a son and a daughter. She lives in Atlanta. He lives in San Francisco. I think they're both retired."

"Then I suggest we go ahead and fly to Santa Fe and investigate that doghouse. I don't know about you, but this makes me want to uncover those fuckers and see them go down. Hard."

"Let's do it. Then maybe we can go to my place and make some plans. Suddenly your 'complicated story' is personal."

Bill and Jake didn't talk much during the flight to Santa Fe. Jake seemed dazed. They landed at Santa Fe Regional Airport in the middle of the afternoon and rented a car. As they pulled out of the airport and headed north to the city's center, Bill called Betty Holden.

"Hi, Betty. We just left the airport. Can we meet at your house in about thirty minutes?"

"That's fine. I'll be there. Rita's house is just down the street from mine."

"Great. See you soon."

"Okay. Bye."

Jake was driving and slowed down for a school crossing.

"You know, Bill, this could be one of the world's great wild goose chases. What the hell are we going to do with that doghouse when we get our hands on it? Tear it apart?"

"If we have to. But maybe there are some gentler first steps. If you see a shopping center with a hardware store or a Walmart, stop. I want to buy a tape measure."

"Okay."

In a mile or so, Jake pulled into a strip mall with a True-Value hardware store. Jake stayed in the car while Bill went in the store. In a few minutes, he returned carrying a retractable tape measure and a short crowbar.

"You gonna measure that doghouse before we tear it apart?

"Elementary, my dear Watson. If Warren hid anything in

the doghouse, it probably would be in a secret compartment. We might be able to find it using the tape measure. You know, outer dimensions versus inner dimensions. If anything's hidden in there, we might be able to get it without tearing the whole doghouse apart."

"I'd be inclined to just bust the thing open."

"My approach might upset Betty less. She's been through a lot lately. She might want to keep the doghouse because Warren built it right before he died. The less damage we do, the better."

"Good point."

Betty greeted them at the front door.

"Come in. A clean-up crew and workers have been here for the past few days. They're gone for the day, but they still have more to do."

Betty was right. The inside of the house was still a mess.

She shrugged.

"It actually looks pretty good now compared to what I found when I returned from Silver City. Warren loved this house. I'm glad he didn't have to see this."

Bill looked out a window into the back yard.

"Betty, is the doghouse still out back?"

"As far as I know. What's all this about the doghouse?"

"The lists that Warren hid in the attic for me don't make a lot of sense in and of themselves. We think maybe Warren left a key to the lists somewhere else. He may have built the doghouse exactly for that reason. Didn't you tell me he insisted on building it, even though Benny never used it?"

"But why all the secrecy if he was just helping you with research on the Middle East?"

"Betty, what I didn't tell you is that what I'm looking into also involves some national security issues. Jake is a former CIA agent. As you know, Warren was close to the intelligence community."

"Did the theft of the file cabinets last year and this break-in have anything to do with that?"

"Possibly. Maybe I should have explained more, but I didn't want to upset you. And, at this point, the less you know the better. When this is over, I'll tell you everything. I hope you understand."

"I do, and I think you're right. Warren used to say the same thing whenever he was involved in something he couldn't talk about. I don't want to know what's going on right now. I just want to sell this house and move to Silver City with Benny and be closer to my sister."

Bill excused himself and went out the front door toward the rented car. Betty and Jake remained in the kitchen. In less than a minute he was back, carrying the tape measure and crowbar.

"Betty, Jake and I are going out back to check out the dog-house. If we have to damage it, we'll do as little as possible. Do you want to come with us?"

"No. Do whatever you need to do. If you find anything, don't tell me. Just take it and leave me in ignorance. I can't take anymore shocks or surprises. In fact, I'm going back to Rita's. When you leave, lock the doors. Are you going to spend the night in Santa Fe?"

"Probably. We flew out here in a private plane and didn't make any return plans. We'll probably drive to Jake's place in Tucson tomorrow. But we don't have any reservations for tonight. We'll wing it. We'll find something."

"Normally, I'd invite you to stay with me. But this is a long way from normal."

"Betty, you've been extremely kind and helpful. If you need anything, don't hesitate to call me. I promise when all this is somehow resolved, we'll get together and I'll explain everything."

"That'll be great. Take care, Bill. You too, Jake."

She reached up and kissed Bill on his left cheek. She shook Jake's hand.

Then she turned, went out the front door and started walking up the street to her friend's house.

Jake turned to Bill.

"Nice woman."

"She sure is. She's been through a lot in the last year. I owe her. We owe her."

"Well, let's check out the doghouse."

The two went into the back yard from the kitchen. The afternoon shadows were starting to get long. The doghouse was sitting next to the patio, about three feet out from the house.

The doghouse had a pitched roof covered with shingles. But unlike other doghouses Bill had seen, the roof wasn't hinged so it could be swung back for cleaning. Using the flashlight on the cell phone, Bill looked inside the doghouse.

"Looks perfectly ordinary. It's obviously never been used."

Jake leaned down to look for himself.

"He used screws instead of nails. Maybe he was a perfectionist. Or wanted to make sure this thing was tight. It's odd the roof isn't hinged. Makes it harder to clean."

"Maybe Warren knew he was never going to clean it."

With the tape measure he bought at the hardware store, Bill measured the exterior dimensions of the doghouse. Then he did the same for the interior.

He turned and look up at Jake.

"What I suspected. The exterior length is four inches longer than the interior length, even accounting for the thickness of the boards. Because of the opening in the front, that extra space has to be in the back."

Jake took the crowbar, stepped to the back of the doghouse, and began trying to pry boards loose. The cross-point screws made it difficult.

"Hold on, Jake."

Bill stepped back into the kitchen and headed for the garage. There, among a box of jumbled tools, he found a

Phillips head screwdriver. He walked back outside and handed it to Jake.

Jake nodded and began to remove the screws holding the back of the doghouse together.

When Bill and Jake were able to pull the boards from the back of the doghouse, they found what they expected: a four-inch deep hidden compartment. Resting in it was a thick manila envelope wrapped in several layers of plastic sealed with gray duct tape.

Bill carefully removed the envelope. He put it on the ground while he and Jake screwed the boards back in place.

"So, what do we do now?"

Jake thought for a few seconds.

"We could drive back to Tucson tonight, but I'm too old and tired for that. We haven't had any lunch and I'm hungry. Plus, it's going to be dark soon, and this house, or its recent history, is beginning to creep me out. Let's try to find a room for the night. That way we can have some dinner and then open this envelope and see if it tells us anything."

"Have you ever eaten at La Fonda Hotel's restaurant?"

"No, but I've heard it's good."

"That it is. Especially the guacamole. Hold on."

Bill called the restaurant and made a dinner reservation for two at seven. He then asked to be switched to reservations and was able to book a double suite for the night.

Jake stepped into the kitchen and put the screwdriver on the counter next to some broken dishes. Bill followed him inside after picking up the envelope, the tape measure, and the crowbar.

"We're set. Let's go."

After dinner, Bill and Jake settled into facing chairs in front of a fireplace in their suite. On a table between them was a bottle of single-malt Scotch whiskey, two glasses, and a bucket of ice. Bill's open laptop was also on the table.

Bill started to open the envelope they retrieved from Benny's doghouse with a pair of scissors from his shaving kit.

Jake poured drinks for them.

"You know what bothers me a bit, Bill, is why would Holden create the lists, leave them for you, and then put the key to them in another place and leave an obscure clue how to find that key?"

"He was very close to the intelligence community and loved talking about spycraft. Maybe he was just playing games. Could be as simple as that."

"I guess. Maybe we'll know more when you get that envelope open."

Bill smiled and cut the last piece of tape away.

Inside the envelope were four eight-by-ten glossy photographs and a thick sheaf of computer paper, each sheet full of single-spaced text.

The photos all had the insignia of NASA on their backs, along with lines of code that meant nothing to Bill or Jake. The back of each picture also had some handwritten notes made with a black felt-tipped pen.

Bill looked closely at the handwriting.

"I'm pretty sure it's Warren's."

"Moon Landing. July 1969." was written under the lines of code on the back of the first picture. In sharp-contrast black and white it showed a wide-angle shot of the Lunar Lander taken from a good distance away.

But it wasn't the Lunar Lander or the moon's surface that caught the attention of Bill and Jake. Hanging in the airless sky, about four of five hundred feet above the landing craft, was a mammoth black, triangular-shaped craft. It was tilted slightly up in the front, so that lights under the craft at the end of each of the triangles were visible. Its size was overwhelming. Each of the three sides was hundreds of feet long.

Jake put his reading glasses on.

"What the fuck is that thing?"

"It's what my friend, Paul Watson, said he saw over his house the night his daughter disappeared."

"A big UFO?"

"Has to be."

"Who took the picture?"

"Neil Armstrong was the first man to step on the moon. Who was the other astronaut with him in the landing module?"

"Buzz Aldrin, I think. There was a third astronaut, but he stayed in the Lunar Orbiter. I can't think of his name."

"So, either Armstrong or Aldrin took the picture?"

"Had to."

Bill put the picture on the coffee table. Both men took a deep sip of whiskey.

Bill picked up the second picture. Both he and Jack recognized it immediately. It was in color, a high-resolution tight close-up the "face" on Mars that had graced the cover of newspapers and magazines around the world when it was released by NASA in 1976. Warren had printed on the back of the photo that it was taken two years ago by a secret mission to photograph the surface of Mars.

Bill looked at Jake.

"Hold on a minute. Something doesn't add up here."

He turned to his laptop and Googled the face on Mars.

"It says here that NASA always dismissed the mile-wide face as a trick of light and shadows. Then, in 1998, this was proved when the Mars Global Surveyor took more photos of the face, and NASA released them to the public. All they showed was a flattened pile of rubble with a vague suggestion of a mouth and eyes. Light and shadows, NASA repeated. The mainstream media lost interest. So how could this picture have been taken two years ago?"

"Unless?"

"Unless what?"

"The 1998 picture of the rubble pile was a fake, and the photo taken two years ago is the real thing."

Jake stood up and refilled their drinks.

"Let's see the other pictures."

The third photo was also of the face, also in color, but it

showed more of the area around it. Sitting in front of the face was a single, black triangular craft that looked very much like the one floating above the Lunar Lander in the first picture. If the face was a mile wide, Bill and Jake figured that each side of the craft was about a quarter of a mile long.

The fourth picture, also in color, was a wider view of the face and the flat plain in front of it. Where the single black triangular object had been in the third photo, there were now eight such objects. They were arranged in a circular formation, looking like a pie whose slices were slightly separated.

Written notes on the back of the third and fourth pictures stated they were also shot two years ago by the same secret mission that had taken the second photo.

Jake cocked his head slightly to the left and took another sip of whiskey.

"What the hell does this mean?"

"I think it means that Colonel West was telling the truth when he said that UFOs and aliens are real. I think these pictures are real. I don't think Warren Holden would have had them if they weren't. He was too smart, too honest, and too tight with the intelligence community for them to be anything but authentic. Somebody slipped them to him. Somebody who knew he was investigating UFOs and The Seven."

"Then the photos prove that the government has been lying all these decades, not only about UFOs but also about the face on Mars. Is there a connection?"

"There must be. Who knows? Maybe the aliens built it thousands of years ago. It could be older than the pyramids. Maybe it was a tribute to some thing or someone. Why were the eight UFOs in a circle formation in front of the face? Maybe it marks the entrance to some underground facility. Remember, West told me the aliens had bases on the moon and Mars. He also said the Seven exists to cover up the truth that the government knows nothing about the UFOs and their occupants, who apparently have been visiting Earth for many thousands of years. He said neither the government nor anyone else has a clue why the aliens are here and why they are interested in us."

"But the government, or The Seven, at least knows they're here. My whole life I suspected they were here. Like Carter and Walter Jansen."

"Well, I have no more doubts either. My only source up to tonight has been Colonel West. These pictures prove we are not alone. We just don't know what it means."

"Let's have a look at those printouts."

Bill picked up the stack of papers, handed the bottom half to Jake, and started reading the first page.

After a few silent minutes, the two men looked at each other. They exchanged stacks of paper. Five more silent minutes went by.

"Holy shit, Bill. Do you realize what this is?"

"I sure do. It looks like a summary of every name on the lists with information about their involvement with The Seven. When they were recruited. What their roles are. What their day jobs are. My God. Look at his. It says that the majority leader of the Senate and the director of the CIA are two of the seven who make up the top leadership. Members of the board, so to speak. Christ, the White House press secretary has a job helping craft The Seven's lies and propaganda. The information on Colonel West fits exactly with what he told me and wrote in his letter. But how do we know all this is authentic?"

"I guess we don't, unless we can confirm some of it ourselves."

"That would be dangerous right now. We're not ready. But I believe these summaries because I trust Warren Holden. He just wouldn't have left something like this if it were bogus."

"What if he also gave copies of the lists, the photos, and summaries to Walter Jansen? And The Seven just got wind of that, maybe from someone at the Carter Center who knew, or suspected, Jansen had them at his house?"

"I think you may be right. That would explain the timing. They took Warren's files a year ago but got nothing because he had stashed the lists in the attic for me. Then a year rolls by and they hear of the summaries. That's when they tossed Betty's house. Again, they found nothing. That could be when they turned to Jansen, knowing he was friendly with Warren. If Jansen had copies of the lists and those summaries and pictures at his house, then The Seven have them. But if they don't know we have them, which is very possible, then we might still be off their radar. But they must worry that they don't have the originals. I wonder how many copies there are. We have the originals of all three. I've made copies of the lists and have them all. Jansen had copies. Is that it?"

"Why didn't Walter tell you about them when you met with him in Atlanta?"

"I don't know. Maybe he wanted you to check me out first. If I passed muster with you, maybe he would have told us both later."

"That would be like Walter. He was a belt-and-suspenders kind of guy. That's one of the reasons Carter trusted him so much."

"Jake, if the top guys in The Seven don't know we have these original lists, summaries, and pictures, then we need to seriously protect them."

Jake gathered up the summaries and photos and stuffed them back into the envelope. He walked over to the closet and put them in the suite's safe.

"We need a four-digit code we'll both remember. In the morning, we'll make photocopies and mail those for safekeeping like you did the original lists."

Bill thought for a few seconds. Then pulled his cell phone out of his pocket and studied its dial pad.

How about 9378? On a phone dial pad, those are the numbers for W-E-S-T."

"Good idea."

Jake punched in the code and locked the safe.

CHAPTER 14

After breakfast, Bill and Jake walked to the UPS store that Bill had used when he copied the lists he found in Betty Holden's attic. They made two copies of the summaries and the pictures, sealed the copies in manila envelopes and overnighted them to George Carson at Eastside Towers in New York and Max Burris at the Post in Washington with instructions to hold them unopened until Bill picked them up.

On the way back to La Fonda, Bill said he wanted to call George and Max Burris to let them know the packets were coming.

"I should have contacted Max when we were in D.C. He's still holding the first packet I sent him with a copy of the lists."

Jake paused.

"You know, maybe we should be more careful with these cell phones. We could be tracked with them."

"Colonel West told me they destroyed my flip phone in hopes that I would get a smart phone that would make it easier to track me. But he also said in the letter that The Seven wasn't paying attention to me anymore. But maybe you're right. Max told me last year in D.C. that nowadays everyone assumes their phones are tapped."

"Welcome to the real world."

"Then I won't call them. I trust both one hundred percent to do as I asked."

At the hotel, they packed, paid the bill at the front desk, and were waiting for the car when Bill tapped Jake's arm.

"Let's not forget to call or stop at the airport and arrange to drop the car off in Tucson instead of here."

"We can just stop at the airport. It's on our way."

"Okay."

∗

It was late when they arrived in Tucson, under a full moon and clear sky. They had eaten dinner on the road and were tired.

Jake suggested they lock the photos and documents in a tall gun safe in his bedroom. Bill agreed. He pulled the envelope out of his backpack and handed it to Jake. Jake wrote the safe's combination on a three-by-five card and handed it to Bill.

"Just in case."

Bill stuck the card in his pocket, smiled, and waved goodnight as he headed out the back door toward the casita, where he fell asleep as soon as he got into bed. But he slept fitfully. He had a jumbled dream about Morgen and UFOs that made no sense. In another dream, Colonel West and Jane were flying together in a black helicopter. In a third dream, he was being chased by Dave Taylor.

He finally got out of bed shortly before seven. He pulled back the curtains to the east-facing picture window and marveled at the mountains in the morning sun. He showered, dressed, and as he started walking toward the main house, he heard splashing from the pool. He walked to the edge and there was Jake swimming laps.

When Jake saw Bill, he stopped swimming and waved.

"I didn't expect you up this early. Did you sleep okay?"

"Not really. I think I was too tired."

"I know. I didn't sleep so well either. My brain wouldn't shut down."

Jake pulled himself out of the water and grabbed a towel hanging on a nearby chair.

"Let me get showered and dressed and then we can have breakfast and return the car to the airport. Unless you want to keep it. But there's no reason for you to. I have a car here."

"Sounds good. I'm hungry."

"Give me fifteen minutes. There's a pot of hot coffee in the kitchen and orange juice in the refrigerator. Help yourself."

"Thanks. I will."

After a breakfast of ham and eggs, the two walked through the house to the garage, which was enormous. Inside was a Mercedes sedan, a Jeep Wrangler, and another vehicle that was covered. Each vehicle had its separate bay and door.

"You drive the rental car and follow me. I know a shortcut to the airport."

Jake pressed a button on the wall and the garage door behind the Mercedes opened. Bill went outside and waited in the rental car until Jake backed out of the garage and pulled around him.

Jake was oddly quiet on the drive back from the airport.

As he pulled into his gravel driveway, he looked over at Bill.

"Bill, I've been thinking about something. It's what kept me awake most of the night. How would you feel about a little road trip and stirring up some trouble?"

"Depends. What do you have in mind?"

"Here's my plan. Let's make seventy-six copies of the photos, the summaries, and the lists and mail a set to every person on the lists. Except Bernard T. Perro and the late Richard West, of course. Let's take the copies and hit the road with them. We'll mail them from different post offices in five or six different states. Little towns. Big towns. We'll even mail a few from Roswell. And let's leave our cell phones here so nobody can trace us. We'll also pay cash for everything, so our credit cards won't give us away. If The Seven is as compartmentalized as we think, I'll bet most of the people on Holden's lists don't know of the others' involvement. They also won't know who on the lists were mailed copies of the lists and pictures. Just them? Some of them? All of them? That ought to set off a shitstorm of paranoia in D.C. It could also be a hell of a lot of fun to watch."

Before Bill could reply, Jake pushed a button on the dash, opening the garage door on the left. He pulled the Mercedes into its bay.

"But even if we ditch our phones, I've read that computers on modern cars allow them to be monitored. Wouldn't The Seven still be able to figure out it was us by comparing our locations with postmarks or whatever the post office uses to keep track of stuff?"

"I'm way ahead of you. Follow me."

Jake walked past his Jeep to the other side of the garage and pulled the cover off the third vehicle.

"Behold! The true love of my life."

There sat a shiny and immaculate car that was bright red and very modern looking.

Bill, like many New Yorkers, didn't own a car and knew little about them.

"What is it? It looks brand new."

"Not even close. It's a 1963 Studebaker Avanti. I spent a bundle restoring it. When it rolled off the assembly line in South Bend, Indiana, it was the fastest production car in the world. They said it could hit more than one-hundred-seventy-eight miles an hour. I've never had the nerve to get even close to that. But its design is what car nuts like me love about it. The fact that your first impression was of a new car is a tribute to the designers. The body is fiberglass. But guess what? No car computers in 1963. Without our cell phones, driving this beauty, and using cash, we're protected from electronic snooping."

"But not inconspicuous."

"True. But if they can't track us, they wouldn't know where to start looking even if they wanted to. And keep in mind, West said you were off their radar now anyway."

"Don't cars this old require leaded fuel?"

"Yes, but I've had this engine modified, so it runs fine on unleaded."

Bill smiled to himself. He had probably just exhausted his knowledge of cars. He decided to change the subject.

"Where are we going to get the cash we'd need? Wouldn't withdrawing a large amount from a bank raise an alert? If we withdraw smaller amounts along the way, we leave a trail."

"Way ahead of you. I keep a wad of cash in my safe as a precaution. I think there's at least ten thousand dollars in there, mostly in twenties and fifties, which should be more than enough to see us through."

Bill thought for a minute.

"Let's do it."

"Pack light. Not a lot of trunk space in this baby."

Bill and Jake spent the next two days getting ready for their road trip.

They made seventy-six copies of the lists and the four photographs, front and back. They used the internet to find the mailing address of the names on the lists. Wearing surgical gloves, they addressed seventy-six manila envelopes using child-like block letters. When they bought the manila envelopes at an Office Max store, they also bought stickers that read "Personal and Confidential." Each envelope got a sticker. There was no return address.

Bill put the envelopes into an Amazon box Jake had kept in a utility room next to the garage. The box fit nicely into the Avanti's trunk. There was just enough room for their suitcases.

They would leave their cell phones, fully charged, on the dining room table, along with the chargers.

"I've got a good friend who lives down the street. I talked to him yesterday, and he's going to come over here every day and take our cell phones for a ride. Some days he'll take both. Other days he'll take one or the other. He'll also keep them charged. That way if someone is tracing them, they won't be suspicious that the phones are in the same place all the time. He'll also make an occasional call from each phone, but always to a number with an automated response, like a movie theater or a big chain pharmacy."

"What else? You're the CIA guy. You know about this stuff."

"Leave your computer here. It can be traced."

"What about credit cards and driver's licenses?"

"I'm pretty sure we're okay with credit cards as long as we don't use them. There is an app that can link a credit card to your cell phone, but we don't have to worry about that since our phones will be here. And I don't even have that app. Do you?"

"Are you kidding? For months I didn't even know how to change my ring tone."

"Driver's licenses could be a problem. They have an RFID chip that can be traced. But I've got a little electronic device I got a couple of years ago from a close friend at the Firm that will block the signal by zapping the chip. We have to have our licenses with us in case we get stopped. We'll also need them to check into a hotel or motel. But they'll be dead electronically. We can both get new licenses later. Just report these as defective."

"What's RFID?"

"It stands for radio-frequency identification. It's used commercially to track all kinds of things."

"You really have thought of everything."

"I hope so. I think we're going to essentially be invisible, which is the whole point. Let's also stay off the interstates as much as we can. We'll enjoy the trip more if we do."

"How long do you think we'll be gone?"

"I'm not exactly sure. If we mail two envelopes from each post office, that's thirty-eight stops. We want to spread the mailing out across several states. Maybe ten days? Two weeks?"

✳

The sun was well up the morning they pulled out of Jake's driveway, the Avanti's trunk loaded with the box of envelopes and their small suitcases. Bill put his backpack in the back seat. Jake had put most of the cash from his safe in a plastic freezer bag that fit snugly under the driver's seat. Their wallets were stuffed with twenties and fifties.

Jake, who was driving, looked over at Bill.

"Well, where to first?"

"I don't know. You pick."

"Let's head west, out through the Arizona desert to Sells and Ajo. From there we can make our way to Yuma and then into California. We'll mail a couple of envelopes from every post office we come across. Then what if we cut north and into Nevada. Maybe we can find a post office near Area 51. That would add a touch of irony. From there we can head east and go to the Grand Canyon. You ever seen the Grand Canyon?"

"Nope. But I always wanted to."

"From the Grand Canyon we could drive on east into New Mexico, then north into Colorado. Maybe Durango. Ever been there? It's a great town."

"Once. Years ago, when I was working in D.C. I don't remember much about it. Isn't there a pretty river that runs through it?"

"Yep, the Animas. Its original Spanish name was Rio de las Animas Perdidas, which means River of Lost Souls."

For the next eleven days, Bill and Jake crisscrossed the Southwest, mailing envelopes from towns big and small. They took turns driving the Avanti, which sometimes drew admiring glances when they stopped for gas or pulled into parking lots. Even though Bill didn't know much about cars, he hadn't forgotten how to drive a stick shift. They mailed the last envelope from the post office in Safford, Arizona, before heading back to Tucson.

CHAPTER 15

The moon was high when they arrived back in Tucson and Jake eased the Avanti into its garage slot. Bill carried his backpack and suitcase out to the casita while Jake took his suitcase and the now smaller bag of money into his bedroom.

A bit later they sat on the patio and shared a bottle of California Merlot.

They both agreed they should check their cell phones for messages but decided to wait until morning.

Bill refilled their glasses and turned to Jake.

"All the envelopes except the ones we mailed in the last three or four days must have arrived by now. What do you think is going on?"

"Hard to know. But my guess is we've caused a lot of anxiety. We need to go to D.C. You can talk to your buddy at the Post and I'll check with my sources. Let's shoot for the day after tomorrow. More envelopes will have arrived, and we'll have time to get things squared away here. We ought to be able to get reservations in the morning. If we can't, we'll charter a plane. I just want to sit here right now and finish this bottle of wine and then go to bed."

"That's fine with me. I'll also check with a good source of mine at the Pentagon when we get to D.C."

Jake was swimming in his pool a little after eight the next morning when Bill started to walk to the main house.

"I'll be there in a couple of minutes. There's coffee and orange juice. Help yourself."

"I will. Thanks."

Later, after a breakfast of cereal and toast, Jake called his neighbor to let him know they were back, and he didn't have to take the cell phones for a drive anymore.

"He's not curious why you asked him to do that?"

"He knows me pretty well. And trusts me. I've done him a few favors. He's not nosy and keeps to himself. He figures I'll probably tell him why later, which I might. Depends on how this all plays out."

Jake got on his laptop and made reservations for flights to Washington the next day. They would have to change planes in Dallas. He then made a five-day reservation for himself at the Mayflower.

He stood up from his computer and poured himself another cup of coffee.

"I assume you want to stay at the Hay-Adams. It's best anyway that we be seen together as little as possible."

Bill nodded and reached for the laptop.

"May I?"

"Of course."

Bill made a reservation for the same five days at the Hay-Adams.

Next, they checked their cell phones for messages.

"Just a couple of messages from my on-again-off-again girlfriend. I'll call her later. If I know her, she's still asleep right now anyway. She was just wondering where I am. We haven't talked in a few weeks."

Bill had two messages from Nancy Luke. Since it was early afternoon in New York, he decided to call her.

"Nancy? I got your messages on my cell phone."

"Hi, Bill. I just wanted to check in with you and see that you're doing okay. Where are you?"

"In Tucson. I should be back in New York in a week or so. We'll have lunch as soon as I get back."

"That'll be fine. I also wanted to let you know that Jack Turner and English-Frostmann are moving right along. I understand they've booked every hotel and motel room within twenty miles of Jefferson. Another thing. I talked to your publisher and arranged for that six-month extension on *Power*

FRED ELLIS BROCK

Points. They weren't happy, but they didn't have a choice."

"Thanks. That takes some pressure off."

"I'll see you in a week or so, then?"

"For sure."

"Bye."

"Bye, Nancy."

Bill also noticed that he had a couple of calls several days apart from a number with an area code he didn't recognize. He used Jake's computer again and discovered that the area code was in Maine. He didn't know anybody in Maine.

He dialed the number and got a recording saying it was no longer a working number. *Probably a robo-call.*

Bill also called the land line at his New York apartment to check for messages. There was a message from his lawyer, Robert Bowers: "Bill, it's Bob Bowers. We need to meet and do something about your will. It's been more than three years since Jane passed, and you still haven't changed it. Please give me a call."

Bill sighed. He knew Bowers was right. *I'll call him as soon as I get back to the city. I guess I've put off changing the will because it would make Jane's death so final. But he's right. It's time. God, I hate the euphemism "passed."*

Jake interrupted Bill's thoughts by filling his coffee mug.

"Thanks. That's good coffee."

"Jamaican Blue Mountain."

"You really are tearing through your father's money."

"I hope so. I want to spend it all. I don't have anybody to leave it to."

"Same here."

"You know, Bill, I've been thinking about something. You feel like talking for a bit?"

"Sure. What's up?"

"I'm not sure what we're going to find in D.C. But it looks like we've been careful enough that we won't be connected to whatever mess we've created, at least not right away. But at some point, we might be. We don't know where this will lead. We need to protect ourselves. There might be a way. My old spook habits die hard."

"What do you mean? I don't understand."

"If The Seven get on to us, they'll kill us. We have to try to protect ourselves from that possibility."

"How?"

"We have to think like terrorist suicide bombers. They strap a bomb around their body, but the detonator is set in reverse. They're holding the button down. The bomb goes off if they release it, not push it. All they have to do to is release the button and BOOM! But that also means if a sniper takes them out, the bomb will go off. Either way, the bomber succeeds. We need to do something like that."

"I'm still not understanding what you're getting at."

"What do we have that could really do damage to The Seven?"

"The lists, the summaries, and the pictures. But now that we've mailed them all over Washington, a lot of people have them. And they could simply say they are fakes, made up stuff."

"But we have something else. The letter from Colonel West. That's not so easy to deny. That letter—along with the lists, summaries, and photos—would be pretty compelling evidence they would have a hard time denying or branding as fake. I just had another thought. Why don't you write a narrative describing everything that's happened to you relative to The Seven since you went to Indiana last year to help your friends. Just write down what you told me."

"That's a good idea. But are you saying we should tell them we have the letter?"

"Sure. Explain it to them but just show enough of it, maybe a few paragraphs, so that they know it's real. They would be able to recognize West's handwriting. Then we tell them that two copies of the letter and the documents, including your narrative, are sealed and being held for us by two different people—four copies in all—with instructions to mail them to The New York Times and The Washington Post if anything happens to either of us or if they try to release the fake file they have on you. The people holding the documents will also mail them if they don't get a call from us once a week at an agreed upon time. The button is down. Harm us and you blow yourselves up."

"But how do we talk to The Seven? You can't just ring them up."

"Well, we know from the summaries that Ross Duncan, the Senate majority leader, and Robert Walker, the director of the CIA, are two of the seven people at the top of the organization. We don't know if there's a chairman of the board, but there probably is. We might have trouble getting through to the CIA director. I was there way before his time, and I don't want to compromise any of my agency contacts by asking them to intervene for me. But the majority leader shouldn't be a problem to arrange a meeting with."

"I know Ross Duncan's press secretary. We used to work together at the Times."

"Then that's where we'll start."

"But won't Duncan suspect we're the ones behind the mailings?"

"Maybe. But if this works, so what? What's he going to do? The mailings will prove that we're a threat, but the West letter should protect us."

"Then what?"

"It buys us time to get organized and gather our forces, as West recommended. It also adds some serious confusion and fear. If Colonel West can turn on them from the grave, might there be others? It also could set back whatever The Seven is planning. A coup?"

"If we go through with this, can we include one other person in our 'button-down' security bubble?"

"Who?"

"Morgen."

"You really are in love with her, aren't you?"

"Yes."

"I guess so. I'm not sure how she'll find out about it. I doubt they would tell her. You said there's no way for us to contact her. We'll just have to wait for her to contact you."

"I suppose. By the way, who are we going to trust with the envelopes to mail if something happens to us?"

"For me, Jim Waters, my neighbor who took our cell phones for a ride. I didn't tell you, but he's a retired cryptographer for the NSA. Top security clearances. He'll do it and won't ask any questions. You?"

"Maybe my lawyer, Bob Bowers, who I just got a phone message from. I've been friends with him for years. He was very fond of Jane. He's also totally reliable. Shouldn't we set this up before we go to D.C.? Or at least before we talk to Duncan?"

"You're right. I jumped the gun on reservations before we talked this through. Tell you what. I'll keep my flight to D.C. tomorrow. You change yours so you can go to New York first and talk to your lawyer. Then we'll meet day after tomorrow in D.C. I should at least have a sense of what's going on by then. That'll give you the rest of today to write the narrative. Is that enough time?"

"I think so. You have a printer, don't you?"

Jake nodded.

"We have to get everything together into two packets, one for Jim Waters and one for your lawyer. There's a photocopy place not far from here that's open till nine. I'll give mine to Jim, and you can take yours to New York tomorrow. Let's agree that I'll call Jim and you'll call your guy every Friday at 3 p.m., give or take ten minutes. If they don't get a call, they mail the envelopes. If we turn up dead for whatever reason, they mail the envelopes."

"What if we're injured in a car wreck and are unconscious? Or what if one of us gets hit by a truck? The other calls his guy, but the one who got hit by the truck can't. One of the envelopes gets mailed, the other doesn't?"

"Yeah, well that's a risk The Seven will just have to take. They better hope we stay well. No system is perfect. Fuck'em."

"I'm glad you were on our side."

✳

Bill was able to switch his flight to New York instead of Washington, but he and Jack were still booked together on the 7 a.m. leg from Tucson to Dallas, where they both had an hour layover. Bill called the Hay-Adams hotel and moved his reservation forward by a day.

It was almost ten when Bill poured another cup of coffee and headed out to the casita and his laptop.

"You can work in here if you want."

"No. I'll be better off out there. Nothing to disturb me."

"If you say so."

It was after four when Bill came back to the main house, holding a flash drive in his right hand.

"Can we print this out?"

Jake led Bill into a small room that was set up as an office. There was a desktop computer and a printer next to it.

Jake inserted the flash drive into the computer, clicked a few keys, and the printer started spitting out twelve pages of single-spaced narration by Bill Sanders.

They took the printed document back to the dining area, where Jake read it after getting them glasses of ice water.

"This is really good. Very compelling. You're a hell of a writer. This, with the West letter, the pictures, the lists, and the summaries makes a pretty convincing set of documents. Let's go to the copy shop. You have the West letter, right?"

"Yes, a copy. In my backpack in the casita."

"We need to select a few paragraphs to copy. This is what we can show Duncan or anyone else to prove how dangerous these sealed enveloped we have placed with other people can be to them. They can see the bomb with the button down."

Bill walked out to the casita and brought back the copy of the letter.

They went through it together and selected two paragraphs and most of a third to photocopy and carry with them to Washington.

Bill read the first one aloud:

When I started working for The Seven, I was a true believer. I believed that the group's original mission, when it was created by Truman, was a noble one: protect the social and economic order. What I came to realize was that by the time I joined, that original mission had long been corrupted. What did you call The Seven? Murder Inc.? Not a bad description. The Seven had become a monster. It has killed hundreds, maybe thousands, of people in order to maintain its secrecy and power. It has violated every law on the books. In a way, it has become what it originally was created to prevent: a broken, lawless society.

He paused, took a drink of water, and read the second:

I'm not sure what the ultimate goal of The Seven is anymore. It operates almost like a secret government. Will its leaders eventually try to take over the government? Stage a coup? I think that's a real possibility, which is why I'm writing this letter to you. I do know this: The Seven has become a greater threat to our social order than if the government were to disclose that UFOs and aliens are real and has no idea why they're here or what they're up to.

Finally, he turned to the partial third paragraph;

... The terrorist attack on the Air France jet that killed your wife was not a terrorist attack. It was a Seven operation from start to finish. Oh, the poor guy who got the bomb on the plane believed he was working for a jihadist group and was headed to paradise and all those virgins. The jihadists that set him up were operatives for The Seven. Their target was a single passenger, a California congressman named James Handforth. He was the chairman of the House Intelligence Committee and was planning to hold public hearings to investigate The Seven. If The Seven had simply assassinated Handforth, there would have been all kinds of investigations. This way was much better from The Seven's point of view. He died simply because he was in the wrong place at the wrong time. No suspicions of anything. No blow-back. Your wife, I believe her name was Jane, was simply what we in the military call collateral damage. As were the other passengers.

Bill choked a bit as he finished reading.

"That was three years ago, right?"

"A little more than. Jane had gone to Paris to visit some friends just before Christmas."

"Well, let's go copy this stuff. We don't need to copy your narrative. We can print copies here. We need copies of the photos, the lists, and summaries. I guess we need to copy the copy of West's letter, since we're going to have to cut it up to get the three paragraphs we want. But you have the original, right?"

"Yes, in my apartment. Plus, a copy in my safe deposit box."

*

It was after six when they returned with the photocopies and two medium- and large-size packages of manila envelopes. They also had a roll of transparent packing tape.

They sorted and packed the copies they had made into four of the smaller envelopes.

"Exactly who do we send these to at the Post and Times?"

"Max Burris at the Post. I guess Gil Stout at the Times. He's the executive editor and knows me well. I'll have to look up the street address of the Post. I know the Times address. I should."

When they were finished, they had two envelopes addressed to Burris and two to Stout. All were taped tight with the packing tape. One copy of the three paragraphs from Colonel West's letter they put into a separate envelope they planned to carry with them to Washington. Jack went to his office and came back with a role of stamps.

"I'm not sure how much postage these will take. Let's just be sure we put on way too much."

Then they stuffed a mailer for Burris and another for Stout into a larger envelope. They repeated this for the second larger envelope. With a black, felt-tipped marker they labeled the first big envelope for Jim Walter, the other for Bob Bowers. They sealed the big envelopes with packing tape.

"I'll run this over to Jim right now. He's to expect a call from us every Friday at 3 p.m. his time, give or take the ten minutes. We agreed on that, right?"

"Right. I'll give mine to Bob when I get to New York tomorrow.

"You like Cajun food."

"Sure."

"There's a good Cajun restaurant about fifteen minutes from here. When I get back from Jim's, let's go eat and then go to bed. We have to get up early in the morning."

"Suits me."

CHAPTER 16

Bill got back to Eastside Towers a little after four. As soon as he walked into the lobby, George waved at him and signaled for him to wait up while he unlocked a drawer in his desk.

"Here's that second envelope you sent me, Mr. Sanders."

"Thanks, George."

Bill pressed a twenty-dollar bill into George's hand.

"Anything exciting happen while I've been gone?"

"Nope. Just the usual."

The first thing Bill did after he let himself into his thirty-second-floor apartment was to put the envelope with the summaries George had just given to him in a desk drawer. He opened his suitcase and put the envelope for Bob Bowers on his bed. Next he opened the curtains and let the afternoon light in. He went into the kitchen and got a diet soda out of his refrigerator. He slowly sipped it as he looked out of his south living room window at the United Nations building and Lower Manhattan.

This is insane. I should be writing, not doing this cloak-and-dagger shit. But I guess I'm in too deep. And those fuckers did kill Jane. And Paul. And Daniel Scott. And Walter Jansen. And a planeload of people, including a congressman.

Bill suddenly remembered he needed to make dinner reservations. He had called Bob Bowers from Dallas and arranged for them to meet at the Italian restaurant Bill liked near his apartment.

He called the restaurant and made reservations for seven.

✳

Bob Bowers had gained a little weight since the last time he and Bill met four months ago. But he was tall and carried it well. The waiter had just delivered two Grey Goose martinis, one of them slightly dirty.

"Bill, I'm sorry to bug you about the will. But you really do need to update it."

"I know. I know. I have to go to Washington tomorrow for a few days. I promise to call you when I get back and we'll take care of it."

"What did you need to see me about that's so urgent?"

"Bob, I have a serious favor to ask that you're going to think is strange. I want you to do something for me without knowing the reason for it. I'll explain it to you later when everything is resolved, but I can't tell you now. I promise you it's nothing illegal or unethical."

"What is it?"

"I have a sealed envelope I want you to hold. Inside it are two other envelopes, addressed, with postage, and ready to be mailed."

"And when am I supposed to mail them?"

"Only under two circumstances. One, if I die or get killed, mail them. Two, I'll call your cell phone every Friday afternoon at three, give or take 10 minutes. If you're not available, I'll leave a message. If you don't get the weekly call or message, mail them."

"Are you in danger? Who'd you piss off? Who the hell are they addressed to?"

"Obviously, you'll find out if you open the big envelope. But I don't want to tell you now. I just want you to trust me."

"You know I do. We've known each other a long time."

"You'll do it, then?"

"Yeah. Somewhat against my better judgment, but I'll do it. I hope I never have to open it. I'd hate to lose a good client, not to mention a good friend. Where's the envelope?"

"I'll drop it off at your office in the morning on my way to Penn Station. Just put it in your office safe and forget about it, unless something happens to me or you don't get a Friday call."

"Right, you said you were going to Washington. How long do you want me to hold this envelope?"

"Not sure. Maybe a few weeks. Maybe a bit longer. I'll know more in a few days."

"Well, I'd like to know what this is about. But I know if you've made up your mind not to tell me, you're not going to."

"But I will. Eventually."

CHAPTER 17

Two military helicopters landed within minutes of each other at the New Mexico ranch. Ross Duncan, the Senate majority leader, and a bodyguard, got out of the first one, surrounded by a whirl of dust. Bent low under the still moving rotor blades, they made their way toward the ranch house. A few minutes later, the second helicopter landed, and Robert Walker, the director of the CIA, stooped into a second cloud of dust and headed for the house, following by a two-man security detail.

Duncan, brushing dust off his suit, was waiting just inside the main door for Walker. Walker paused, pulled a handkerchief from his pocket, and wiped his face and the arms and front of his suit. Then, without a word, they walked past a conference room and headed for the elevator. The three guards stayed by the door.

Three stories below ground, it was cool and quiet. The two continued in silence down a carpeted, dimly lighted corridor toward a larger conference room. Five other people—two woman and three men, all casually dressed—were seated at a large conference table. They rose as Duncan and Walker entered. Duncan took the chair at the head of the table. Walker sat to his right.

Duncan looked around the room.

"I trust everyone got the message. I mean everyone. Snakebite is on hold, and Lockdown is in effect until we figure out what the hell is going on. Who in the name of Christ got a copy of those lists and summaries, not to mention the pictures? They must have had them before we found them in

Jansen's house. I thought neutralizing him would end it. Son of a bitch! They mailed them to everybody on the lists, including me and Walker, from all over the West. If we hadn't ordered the Lockdown procedure, this could have been a disaster. Luckily, the lists weren't even close to complete, so they didn't totally destroy the compartmentalization we spent years building."

One of the women at the table spoke up.

"This may not be as bad as we think. Look, as long as this stuff doesn't cause any internal disruption, we can always deny everything. If it gets out, we can blame it on UFO kooks and conspiracy theorists. Offer proof that the pictures were faked. NASA can do that for us. The lists and summaries are the products of sick minds out to undermine the government. Maybe the Russians or the Chinese are behind it. We have lots of options."

Walker looked at the woman.

"Unless there is more to come."

"Meaning?"

"What if these mailings create dissention in the ranks? What if those who got them get suspicious of those who didn't? What if someone gets nervous and starts talking out of school?"

Duncan held up his right hand in a gesture of silence.

"Let's not get ahead of ourselves. We may never know who mailed these damn things. Or who else has copies. If they're leaked, we can deny everything, but the Lockdown is hopefully going to make that unnecessary. What more could there be? And who the hell is Bernard T. Perro?"

Everyone shook their heads at the last question.

Duncan turned and looked directly at Walker.

"Bob, do we have any indication the White House is involved in any way."

"No. I spoke to the President recently. I can guarantee he knows nothing. Anyway, if he did, our guy inside the White House would have alerted us."

Walker nodded and turned his gaze toward a man seated at the end of the table.

"Last time we met, I suggested keeping a loose eye on that writer, Bill Sanders. Did we find out anything that should concern us?"

"No. Not at all. Until recently, he was out of the country for an extended time. He's got a fat contract for a book he's working on about the Middle East, and he was over there doing research. After he returned to the U.S., he visited Walter Jansen at the Carter Center. But he was obviously interviewing Jansen for his book. The Mideast was one of Jansen's areas of expertise when he was in the White House."

"But wasn't Sanders trying to visit Jansen a year ago when West blocked the bridge in Louisville?"

"Yes, but we're pretty certain this aborted visit was book-related and had nothing to do with us or events in Indiana last year. Just another screw-up by West's team. After all, Sanders acquiesced and kept silent after West showed him the file we put together. We know of nothing that would indicate he has changed his mind. He's smart and has too much at stake to see his reputation ruined."

"Anything else?"

"Sanders visited Warren Holden's widow a couple of times in Santa Fe, but we're pretty sure that, too, was in connection with his book. Remember, Holden was a major source for his book on South America, and they were friends. Holden was also close to the intelligence community and had more than a passing knowledge of the Middle East. We think Sanders may have been looking for some files on the Mideast that he thought Holden had. Or maybe he was interviewing Mrs. Holden. Or both. Unfortunately for him, we took the file cabinets long before he got there. They did, by the way, have a bunch of files on the Mideast. We destroyed them along with everything else in the file cabinets after we found nothing of interest to us."

The man paused and then continued.

"Sanders also linked up with a retired CIA guy in Tucson named Jake McCoy."

Walker looked up.

"He's been retired from the agency for a long time."

"Yes, I know. But he was assigned to the White House during Carter's last year in office. He had been stationed in the Mideast earlier, and he became friends with Walter Jansen. We think Jansen suggested that Sanders talk with McCoy. Again, about the Mideast for the book."

"You have tracking data on all this?"

"Oh, sure. Thank heaven for smart phones. We know neither Sanders nor McCoy could have been involved in mailing those lists and summaries because during the time they were mailed both men were in Tucson. They were either at McCoy's house or around Tucson at restaurants and even a couple of movie theaters."

Duncan sighed.

"What about Morgen Remley? Any problems with her?"

"No. As you said, she's solid. She's working on a project to discredit a couple of academics who are asking too many questions."

"Where is she?"

"In Maine. Portland."

CHAPTER 18

Bill stopped at Bob Bowers' law office on Park Avenue a little before ten the next morning. He made sure to put the envelope directly in Bowers' hand. Bowers insisted Bill watch him lock it in an office safe.

"Thanks, Bob. I really appreciate this."

"I just hope I get a call from you at three every Friday."

"So do I."

From the law office, Bill took a taxi to Penn Station and boarded an Acela train for Washington. Two hours and forty-five minutes later he walked out of Union Station and caught a taxi to the Hay-Adams Hotel.

Once in his room, he texted Jake: "I'm here."

Seconds later, a reply: "Stand by."

Within thirty minutes Jake was seated in Bill's hotel room. He looked worried.

"I've got good news and less good news. I got lucky yesterday and made contact with an old agency friend who has a brother-in-law at the State Department who likes to hit the bottle. About a month ago, this guy had way too much Jack Daniels and started blabbing to my friend about his ties to this secret group called The Seven. Said they were very powerful and were planning something big. Then he clammed up. My buddy figured it was just the ramblings of a drunk blowhard and didn't think much about it until I started questioning him and asked if he had ever heard of The Seven. Now he's got some feelers out for me. I guess in a way it's some confirmation of what Colonel West told you and wrote in his letter."

"What's the less good news?"

"We've got to change our plans. Remember earlier I said that people I had talked to sensed something big was about to happen, like animals sensing an earthquake."

"Yes. And?"

"There's been a sudden calm that followed us mailing those envelopes. We expected a shitstorm. We got the opposite. Everybody has gone silent. I think the minute those envelopes started hitting, The Seven must have put out the word: Ignore them. Don't speak of them. Destroy them. Pretend they never existed. I also suspect that whatever they were planning—a coup or whatever—has been put on hold for a time. I don't think The Seven has any idea who sent those mailings. They only went to seventy-six people. How many are involved with The Seven? Thousands, as West said? How many of those are in D.C.? How is the military involved? What we did was to throw some sand in the gears. Enough to slow things down for a time, but that's all."

"So why do we have to change our plans?"

"Because if we go to Duncan with the partial West letter and the threat of someone mailing those packets to the press if anything happens to either of us, he'll simply pretend not to know what we're talking about. They won't try to harm us, and they'll say they know nothing. All those people we mailed the envelopes to will say they never got them, that they don't know what we're talking about. Then what do we do? Try to go public. It won't work. And we will have exposed ourselves. We will have done what West warned us not to do. We will have moved too quickly to the center without gathering enough evidence and building enough support first. What did West say? Work discreetly and gather our forces. Get powerful people on our side. Going directly to Duncan will be jumping the gun. Right now, I don't think they have any idea of our involvement. The minute they do, we have to be protected. The threat of having those packets mailed might do it, but as I've been thinking about it, I've come to the conclusion that we also need some powerful forces on our side. We can't let The Seven know that we're onto their plans without first making sure the powers that be also know it and are working with us. Otherwise, we're out on a limb."

"The powers that be? We know the CIA director and the President's press secretary are involved. Where do we turn?"

"I'm not sure. Maybe the President himself. West said he wasn't involved. Maybe the military, or those in the military we can be sure of. At any rate, we've got to gather more evidence and pull in allies."

"I see your point. So, what next, if not Duncan?"

"Again, what West said. Be cautious and marshal our forces. I'm going to keep talking to some old D.C. contacts. Why don't you get in touch with your friend at the Post and your old source at the Pentagon and see what you can discover from them?"

"How much do we want to tell them?"

"At this point, I'd say whatever it takes to get them on our side. Things could start moving fast."

"Well, I'll set up a meeting with Max and try to contact my Pentagon source. You want to meet later tonight for dinner?"

"Good idea. Let's eat here. That steak I had the last time we were here was great. What's the restaurant called?"

"The Lafayette. They also have a great rack of lamb. I'll make a reservation for eight."

"Perfect."

"Max Burris."

"Max, it's Bill Sanders. I'm in D.C. How about breakfast tomorrow?"

"Sure. It's been a while."

"A year. Is eight okay?"

"Yep. See you then."

They always met at the same place, the Sunrise Coffee Shop. Bill had learned when he contacted Max last year that it was wise not to include a lot of details in phone calls these days, something events and Jake had reinforced.

Bill made his reservation for dinner with Jake and then texted Larry Summers at the Pentagon: "It would be great to see you again."

Seconds later came the reply: "Tomorrow 2 p.m."

Colonel Lawrence Sullivan worked in Army intelligence, where he had spent most of his military career. He and Bill had become friends when Bill worked for The New York Times in Washington; Larry soon became an important and highly confidential source for Bill, which resulted in a number of hard-hitting stories that became an important part of Bill's reputation as a top reporter. Larry fully trusted that Bill would never expose him as a source. He knew Bill would go to jail rather than break his confidence. Bill knew it, too. Luckily, it never came to that.

When Bill left the Times to write books, he and Larry drifted apart over the next decade. But Bill, with help from Max Burris, contacted Larry last year when he was looking for the mysterious Richard West, and the years evaporated as Larry secretly helped him again. At the time, Bill promised at some point to explain why he was looking for West.

Now, a year later, Bill needed his help again. He knew he might have to explain West.

Their one-sentence code—"It would be great to see you again."—usually required no response. It meant they would meet at a prearranged spot in exactly one hour. The only time a response was necessary was if the meeting was at another time. The rendezvous was always at the entrance to the Elephant Trails exhibit at the National Zoo.

Bill and Jake were seated in a quiet corner of the restaurant. They had ordered martinis and were waiting for them to arrive.

"Did you contact Burris and your Pentagon source?"

"I'm meeting Burris for breakfast in the morning and my

source in the afternoon. How'd things go with you."

"Strange. Very strange."

"How? What do you mean?"

"Remember yesterday I said things had gone quiet? That's true. But there's also something in the ether I've never felt before: fear. No, not exactly fear. It's a kind of weirdness that's hard to explain. It's like people aren't sure what to think anymore. They're apprehensive and don't know exactly why. People they've known for years are suddenly acting differently. It's like people are afraid of something but don't know what it is. Take my friend with the State Department brother-in-law who drinks too much. When I mentioned The Seven and he connected it to what his brother-in-law had said, I could see fear, or this weirdness, creep into the corners of his eyes. He agreed to help, to put out feelers. But he's nervous. Of what? I'm not sure. I'm not sure he knows. It can't be the coup West said The Seven is planning. They're too compartmentalized and tightly controlled to let that leak. It's got to be something else."

"Why didn't you just ask your friend?"

"I almost did. But I held back because I didn't want to spook him. No pun intended. But the main reason is that I didn't think much about it at the time. It was only later in the day when I picked up the same look in the eyes of a couple of other people I talked to when I mentioned The Seven that I started putting two and two together."

"Could that be because of Walker?"

"I don't think so. The director's role in The Seven has to be one of the most closely guarded secrets in the world. Even if it did leak, it wouldn't cause the kind of thing I'm picking up. These guys I'm talking to are long-time, hardened agents. They may have heard some scuttlebutt about The Seven. But its existence—even its plans for a coup—isn't something that would trigger fear in these men. Anger, maybe. Not fear."

A waiter arrived with their drinks and took their dinner orders. Both had the rack of lamb, medium rare. They agreed on a bottle of Cabernet Sauvignon.

When their waiter had left, Bill took a sip of his martini and looked at Jake.

"Jake ... this fear thing or whatever you're picking up. Maybe it's a simple fear of being killed or blackmailed, like I was. I mean, hell, The Seven has stacked up quite a few bodies in my case."

"Yeah, but these guys wouldn't know about that. Only the reporter and Walter Jansen were officially listed as homicides. You're the only one who knows of their link to The Seven and of the truth of the death of your friend and his daughter. And the earlier deaths of the people on your wife's plane."

"At least one other person knows."

"Who?"

"Morgen. West said in his letter to me that he sent her a letter like mine."

"She wouldn't be spreading fear among people in D.C. We don't know where she is or how to contact her. If you love her, you must trust her.

"I do. I guess you're right. Let me see what I pick up tomorrow from Burris and my Pentagon source."

CHAPTER 19

Bill was getting dressed the next morning, preparing to meet Max Burris for breakfast, when his cell phone rang. It was Jake.

"Good morning, Jake."

"Have you heard the news?"

"No. Why."

"My friend's alcoholic brother-in-law who was blabbing about you know what?"

"What about him?"

"He was killed by a hit-and-run driver near the Kennedy Center last night around eleven. And get this. The car that hit him, a brand-new Cadillac, was found abandoned ten blocks away. It had been stolen a few hours earlier from a dealer's lot in Maryland. Police think the driver had arranged to be picked up there by someone in another car. Sound familiar?"

"Jesus. It's them all over again. The second car will probably turn up later. It's the bridge in Louisville and Walter Jansen all over again."

"Look, Bill, go ahead and meet with your two guys. I'll see what I can pick up, and we'll meet for dinner. I have a place in mind. I'll leave a message at your hotel."

Jake is nervous. I hear it in his voice. And he didn't want to mention the restaurant over the phone.

Bill was just getting seated at a table in the Sunrise Coffee Shop when Max arrived. They gave each other a bear hug.

Max's black hair had a few more streaks of gray; his dark eyes were as intense as always. Max handed Bill two manila envelopes.

"You wrote I should hold these for you. Here they are. Should I be curious?"

Bill slipped them into his backpack.

"I'll explain later."

"Okay. By the way, last year you said you would buy me dinner in New York when the royalties started rolling in from that novel."

"Still will. All you've got to do is come to New York."

"I will. Maybe later in the summer."

"I'll be there. Working my butt off on my Mideast book. I'm more or less finished with research and interviews. I recently got back from spending several weeks in Beirut, Tel Aviv, and Cairo. Then I was here for a few frantic days finishing up some interviews. I meant to get in touch with you then, but I was just too busy."

"I hear you. What's up? Anything new?"

"Max, this is a little awkward and you may think I'm crazy. But I've gotten myself involved in something that may turn out to be a very big story. I need your help. In return, you can have the story."

A waitress interrupted them with two mugs of steaming coffee.

"I'm Molly. I assumed you wanted this. Cream and sugar are on the table. You want to order breakfasts now or should I come back in a couple of minutes?"

Bill ordered pancakes and bacon. Max decided on bacon and scrambled eggs with hash browns.

Molly wrote down their orders, turned, and headed toward the kitchen.

Max sipped his coffee black. Bill added some cream.

"What kind of story?"

"That's the problem. I'm still trying to figure it out. And I need your help to do that. But I want you to help me without knowing a lot of the details up front. In time, you will. But if I tell you everything I know, I'm afraid you might not believe me. Or if you do believe me, you might do something rash."

"Bill, you were one of the best reporters I've ever known. What could you possibly tell me that would make me think you were lying or crazy?"

"I appreciate that, but I have to do this my way. It's personal. I'm involved. I'm not a neutral reporter on this. It's very strange, complex, and convoluted. I want to move you into it slowly at first. I don't want to overwhelm you with too much weird information. In addition, I know what a damn good reporter you are. If I tell you everything I know at once, you'd likely just rush off and start writing a story. Same as I would if I were in your place. I understand that. But that can't happen right now for reasons that will become clear to you. You also have to swear that everything we discuss is just between us until we decide you can go public. Will you do that? Will you help me?"

Max started to reply just as Molly showed up to offer them more coffee, which they both accepted.

"Well, you sure drive a hard bargain. But your offer intrigues me. Mainly because I know you well enough and trust you enough to believe you must have something big, and your reasons for how you want to play it are probably valid. So, where do we start?"

"Have you ever heard of an organization called The Seven? Capital T, capital S."

Max's left eye twitched, almost imperceptibly.

"That's the second time in a week I've heard a reference to The Seven. What the hell is it?"

"What was the first time?"

"Last Thursday, I think. There's an older editor who sits in the cubicle next to mine. Leon Jenkins. A solid guy but not very friendly, although I get along with him better than most. Anyway, I was at my desk when I noticed him leave his cubicle and head for the mail room. In a few minutes he returned with a stack of mail. I didn't pay any more attention to him, although I could hear him using a knife that he kept on his desk to open his mail. He was ripping envelopes open. Then thing got quiet. Suddenly, I heard him moan, 'Oh, fuck!' I thought he was sick or something and started to get up and check on him. Then I heard him pick up his phone headset and punch in a number. He started talking very low. I couldn't really hear what he was saying, but I did hear him say what sounded like 'the seven.' I figured maybe he was talking to his bank or tax guy. You know, 'carry the seven' or something. I didn't think anything more about it and went back to my computer. A few seconds later I heard his chair squeak as he stood up. I turned around just in time to see him, carrying a thick manila envelope, head toward the office cross-cut shredder. He returned in a couple of minutes empty-handed. We never spoke a word. I had actually forgotten about this. Then you show up today and ask if I've ever heard of The Seven. What the hell is this all about? Who or What is The Seven? What the hell is going on?"

"Did you see the story about the State Department guy who was killed by a hit-and-run driver near the Kennedy Center last night."

"Yeah. It was in the late edition. Why?"

"He was killed by The Seven."

"What!"

"So was Walter Jansen in Atlanta."

Molly suddenly appeared with their plates of food.

"Can I get you anything else?"

"Some syrup for my pancakes."

"Oh, sorry."

She was back with a small pitcher of warm syrup in less than a minute.

"Just wave at me if you need anything else."

Molly turned and headed in the kitchen.

"What do you mean he was killed by The Seven? And Walter Jansen? What is it, some kind of Mafia outfit?"

"Bear with me. First, I need your read on something. I've been hearing indirectly that the D.C. intelligentsia is on edge, filled with unexplained apprehension that something big is about to happen. Have you sensed that?"

"Absolutely. A lot of people hinted at it, but nobody could put their finger on it. Then ...."

"Like when animals can sense an earthquake coming before it strikes?"

"Exactly."

"I interrupted you. You were about to say?"

"I was going to say that a few days ago, everything went silent. A lot of people clammed up. They didn't return phone calls. It's been bizarre."

"It may have to do with The Seven. Max, what do you know of, or think of, UFOs? Unidentified Flying Objects. Some people, especially the military, call them UAPs, for unidentified aerial phenomena."

"Where the hell is this going? What do UFOs have to do with The Seven and a hit-and-run death?"

"Humor me. I want to work into this slowly, sometimes from the side. You'll see why soon enough. UFOs?"

"Oh, hell. Okay. I don't think much about UFOs unless they get into the news in a fairly big and unavoidable way. Those Pentagon disclosures about military pilots sighting UFOs and recording radar images of them caught my attention. Every now and again there's something about Roswell. But trying to figure out what happened there so many years ago is like trying to figure out who killed JFK. I was also intrigued to learn that Harry Reid, when he was the Senate majority leader, convinced the Pentagon to spend twenty-two million investigating UFOs. After he left office, Reid gave an interview in which he said he believed in extraterrestrial life."

"What do you believe? What do you think is the government's role in all this?"

"I don't have any convictions much one way or the other. I think most sightings are bullshit. But I suspect the government knows more than it's telling. Twenty-two million dollars is a lot of money to throw at something you don't think is real. Why are we even talking about this?"

"Because at the end of the Second World War, Harry Truman established an ultra-top-secret group to investigate UFOs and control the public perception of them. The group was called The Seven because of the number of its top members, its board of directors so to speak."

"I thought the group Truman supposedly created was called Magic something or another. But wasn't the document establishing it proven to be a fake?"

"Majestic 12. The document wasn't 'discovered' until 1984. But the whole Majestic 12 story was bogus from beginning to end. The Seven created the Majestic 12 document so it could later be discredited along with the whole idea of a secret group having been established by Truman. Great cover for The Seven."

"How do you know all this? I had no idea you were into UFOs and secret organizations."

"I wasn't. Then something happened last year. In Indiana."

"What?"

"A friend's ten-year-old daughter was abducted by a UFO. She was later kidnapped and killed by The Seven."

"Bill, stop. This is getting crazy. I trust you, but this is too much. I've got to get to work. Maybe we'll talk later."

Max tossed a twenty-dollar bill on the table and left.

Bill signaled Molly for another cup of coffee.

I guess I screwed that up. But I'm not sure how I could have played it differently. The whole story at once? A litany of The Seven's murders? The photos, lists, and summaries? The threat of a coup? His reaction might have been even more negative. I can't really blame him. I guess I know how he feels. I remember how I felt when Paul first told me that he witnessed Cindy being abducted by a UFO. I hope I haven't lost a friend.

Bill finished his coffee, added another ten dollars to Max's twenty, left the Sunrise Coffee Shop, and walked slowly back to the Hay-Adams. Once in his room, he opened one of the envelopes Max had given him and pulled out the lists. There on the page labeled Washington Post was the name Leon Jenkins. Bill stuffed the list back into its envelope and locked both envelopes in his room safe. He was careful to make the safe code 9378.

*

At two o'clock Bill was sitting on a bench in front of the National Zoo's Elephant Trails exhibit.

The more I think about it, the more I realize I handled that meeting with Max badly. Maybe I should have just shown him the pictures and Colonel West's letter to start with.

"Hey, stranger."

Bill looked up to see Larry Sullivan standing next to him. He was wearing khaki slacks and a dark blue polo shirt. His reddish blond hair and freckles gave him a boyish look.

Bill jumped up and they shook hands.

"Thanks for showing up. Is this how they dress in the Pentagon these days?"

"No. I'm off today. Had a doctor's appointment this morning."

"Nothing serious, I hope."

"Nope. Just a follow up on a kidney infection I had last month. I'm fine now. So, what's up?"

"Larry, I need your help again. Same deal. I'll go to jail before I reveal you as a source."

"I know and believe that. I wouldn't be here if I didn't."

"Remember last year when I asked you to help me find a Colonel Richard West? You said the lid was really tight on him, and you referred me to a doctor in Brussels who had known him when he was there with NATO."

"I remember. But didn't I read last year that West died? I remember wondering if you ever found him."

"I did. Or rather, he found me. Anyway, I did make contact with him before he died."

"Did he help you with whatever you were looking for?"

"Yes and no. I promised last year to explain it all to you, and I will. Just not now. What I need now is another favor."

"What is it?"

FRED ELLIS BROCK

"Have you ever heard of an organization called The Seven?"

"No, I don't think so. Should I have?"

"Not necessarily. What I want you to do is poke around and see what you can find out about The Seven. But be careful. They're a secret group, and they're dangerous. Only talk to people you know and trust."

"Are they some sort of reactionary paramilitary group or something?"

"I'm not sure. Just be careful."

"This may take a couple of days. Where are you staying?"

"The Hay-Adams. One more thing."

"What?"

"What's your sense of what's going on these days? I don't mean specific things. I mean impressions and feelings. What's in the air? Anything unusual or odd?"

"Funny you should ask. Early last week a friend of mine at work and I were talking about the fact that there seemed to be a lot of tension in the air. A feeling that something big was about to happen. There was a lot of activity and chatter. We figured there was an invasion in the works, maybe in the Middle East again. Then suddenly, and for no discernable reason, things got very quiet. They're still quiet. Weirdly so. Nobody wants to talk or speculate about anything. Suddenly everybody is very formal and cautious at meetings. That could be a problem for me trying to find out something about The Seven, but I'll do what I can."

"I know you will. What you describe fits with something else I heard. Anyway, do what you can on The Seven but be careful. I promise you'll get the full story before too long."

"I'll be in touch."

With that, Larry turned and walked away.

✳

When Bill got back to the hotel, there was a note from Jake at the front desk: "Pearl's Chinese Palace. 7 p.m." There was no address.

Bill asked the concierge for directions and discovered the restaurant was only seven blocks from the Hay-Adams.

"Pearl's has been open less than a year, and it's gotten rave reviews. A friend told me the lobster with black bean sauce is out of this world."

"Thanks. I'm looking forward to it."

Once in his room, Bill decided he had time to take a short nap before getting ready for dinner. He called the front desk and ask for a wake-up call in an hour.

It was dark and cold. Bill and Morgen were hungry. They had left the airliner crash site but were now lost in deep woods. They held each other close for warmth and kept walking, following a vague path that meandered among huge trees. Suddenly they came to a small clearing, totally surrounded by trees. In the center of the clearing was a log cabin, its lights filling every window. Smoke curled from a brick chimney. The cabin looked warm and welcoming. Bill and Morgen started walking toward it.

Bill stopped. He realized the cabin was Paul's. But it should be in Indiana, not here in the middle of these woods. Morgen took his hand and pulled him toward the cabin.

"It's okay, Bill. We'll be safe there."

"But how did Paul's cabin get here?"

"It's not important. Come on."

The front door opened, and a man stepped out. It was Richard West! He was wearing the same dark brown, three-piece suit and green tie that he had been wearing when Bill first met him more than a year ago.

"Hello, Bill. Morgen. Welcome. You look tired and hungry."

"You're dead."

"Come now, Bill, let's not get hung up on technicalities. Come inside. We've been expecting you."

"We?"

Without another word, Colonel West motioned them inside. There, in front of a roaring wood fire, was a dining table covered with steaming platters of food. The smell of the wood fire mingled with the aroma of roast beef and fresh baked bread.

Bill did a double take. Sitting at the head of the table was Jane! She smiled gently at Bill, who was speechless.

Jane stood up, walked across the room and stood next to Colonel West.

"You two go ahead and eat. Richard and I have to leave now."

As though someone had turned on an overhead stage light, the outside of the cabin was suddenly bathed in blinding while light. Jane and Colonel West turned and walked out the door into the clearing. Bill and Morgen followed.

There in the clearing was a shaft of blue light. Bill looked up. It and the white light were coming from a gigantic triangular craft overhead.

Jane touched Bill's cheek with her right hand and smiled at him again. Then she and Colonel West stepped into the blue light. Immediately, as if by magic, they began to rise and disappeared into the bottom of the craft. The white and blue lights blinked off, and the craft silently disappeared into the night sky.

It was cold and dark again. When Bill and Morgen turned around, the cabin and clearing were gone. They were still in the deep woods. Bill fell to his knees, filled with sorrow, and started to cry. He looked around. Morgen was gone. Vanished. His sorrow turned to terror.

Bill blinked awake in a cold sweat and a panic. He closed his eyes and tried to calm down. He looked at his watch. Five-thirty.

The bedside phone starting ringing.

"Hello."

"Good afternoon, Mr. Sanders. This is your five-thirty wake-up call. The weather is clear and eighty-two degrees."

"Thanks."

"Have a good rest of your day."

Bill lay back on his pillow. He felt drained. The dream was still sharp in his memory.

What in God's name was that all about? Morgen and Jane together in another dream. And West! And Jane is taken away in a spaceship with him! Paul's house. With a table and all that food, which vanished along with the house. And Morgen. Also vanished. Maybe this whole business is putting me under too much pressure. Maybe I should vanish for a while.

After a few more minutes, Bill got out of bed and took a long, hot shower. He felt better.

He picked up the phone and called the concierge.

"This is Bill Sanders. You gave me directions this afternoon to Pearl's. Is it formal? Do I need a jacket and tie?"

"No, Sir. Business casual is fine."

"Great. Thanks."

"No. Problem. Enjoy your dinner."

Bill put on some khaki slacks, a blue dress shirt with an open collar, and cordovan loafers. He had a little time to kill and decided to walk to the restaurant.

Jake was seated at a corner table and looking at the menu when Bill arrived. They shook hands, and Bill picked up his menu. Jake was subdued and had a worried look on his face.

A white-jacketed waiter took their orders for Tsingtao beer.

"Is something wrong?"

"I'm not sure. Maybe. How was your day?"

"Well, I struck out with Max Burris. He walked out on me at breakfast. Found the whole thing too weird. I'll call him tomorrow and try a different approach. I'm thinking of showing him West's letter and the other stuff, including the photographs. I probably should have done that to start with. However, I did learn one interesting thing from Max. When I first mentioned The Seven, he said that was the second time he had heard the term in a week. Turns out Max overheard an editor named Leon Jenkins in an adjoining cubicle say 'the seven' during a phone call he made last Thursday right after he got his mail. Then he shredded a thick manila envelope he had received. Max didn't think anything of it until I asked him if he had ever heard of the Seven. By the way, Leon Jenkins is one of the names on the lists."

"That's confirmation, I guess, that Holden wasn't blowing

smoke. What about your military guy?"

"My Pentagon source is working his contacts. I'll hear from him in a day or so."

The waiter arrived with their beer and took their orders. Both had some hot and sour soup. Bill decided on the lobster with black bean sauce. Max ordered shrimp fried rice.

"I guess I had better luck than you did. I talked to three agency guys I know and trust one hundred percent. Our little mailing campaign may have had more impact than we thought. It's true that whatever was in the works that people sensed suddenly went quiet when our envelopes started arriving. It's still quiet, but there are leaks around the edges of The Seven's compartmentalization and tight control. Those mailings scared some people. Made them very nervous. The CIA director and the Senate majority leader both left town separately a few days ago, supposedly to meet up in New Mexico to go fly fishing. We know The Seven keeps people in line through fear and blackmail. It worked for a while with you. If not for your relationship with Morgen it might still be working. Maybe our mailings unnerved some people enough that they realized they didn't want to be a part of whatever the group had become or was planning to do. Death gave West an easy way out of The Seven. But would he have written that letter if he weren't dying?"

"I don't think so."

"Me neither. But everyone's not the good soldier that West was. Our mailings exposed and widened some cracks in The Seven."

"Are your people talking about it?"

"Not in so many words. Though things have gone quiet, there's a lot of close-to-the-vest gossip about a secret group that's planning something. Two of the guys I talked to today said they had friends who had suddenly become very nervous and withdrawn. I think they got our envelopes."

The waiter arrived with two steaming bowls of hot and sour soup.

"Will that be all for now? More beer?"

Both nodded and the waiter took their empty bottles and glasses.

"You said earlier you thought something might be wrong. What did you mean?"

"I'm worried that the people who run The Seven might sense the ground shifting under their feet and do something rash. They might step up the process of killing people they don't trust. Or they might change the timetable for whatever they're planning. A coup? Maybe try to stage it sooner rather than later. I know how these kinds of people think. They've had things pretty easy up to now. But those events in Indiana involving you didn't go so well for them. And now our mailings."

Their second round of Tsingtao arrived, along with their main courses.

They were just starting to eat when Bill's cell phone rang. He looked at it. The caller was Max Burris.

"Hey, Max. I'm glad to hear from you. Hope you're not too upset with me."

"Bill, I have to see you now. Tonight. At your hotel. It's important."

"I'm having dinner with a friend at Pearl's. I could be back at the hotel in an hour. Can my friend join us? We've been working together on what we discussed at breakfast."

"I guess. Sure. What's your hotel?

"The Hay-Adams."

"I'll be there. One hour. Bye."

Jake took a sip of beer.

"What was that all about?"

"It was Max. He wants to see me right away. He's upset about something. You're invited. Before we go, I need your opinion. I trust Max. I'm going to come clean with him. Tell him everything, which is what I should have done this morning. But should I tell him about the envelopes that we mailed? Should I tell him we're the culprits in that caper?"

"You really trust him?"

"Yes. Absolutely."

"Then tell him. We'll be doing what West said. Starting at the outer edges of this thing."

CHAPTER 20

When Bill and Jake walked into the lobby of the Hay-Adams, Max was waiting for them. He was obviously nervous and upset as Bill introduced him to Jake.

"What's so important?"

"Let's go up to your room so we can talk privately."

Bill pointed toward the elevators.

Once the three were in Bill's room and sat down, Max relaxed a little.

"What's going on, Max? What's so important? I was afraid you might not speak to me again after our meeting at breakfast."

"It's Leon Jenkins."

"The editor you mentioned this morning?"

"Yes."

"What about him?"

"He's dead. Killed by a hit-and-run driver not far from the office at a little before four this afternoon. He usually left the office about that time most days to get a sandwich and coffee from a take-out place across the street that he liked. He was on his way back across the street when it happened. Eyewitness told police that a big sedan swerved out of its lane and ran him down."

Bill and Jake exchanged glances. Bill turned to Max.

"Was the car found abandoned a few blocks away? And was it a new car, recently stolen from a dealer's lot?"

"Yes, but ...."

"Think back, Max. Remember the State Department guy we talked about who was killed last night near the Kennedy

Center? Same kind of operation. A brand-new car, stolen and abandoned. A second car must have been waiting to pick up the hit-and-run driver. That second car will probably turn up abandoned somewhere in a day or so. It's a method they use over and over again because it's so successful. Walter Jansen was killed the same way in Atlanta. It's almost foolproof."

"Who is 'they'?"

"The Seven. I was trying to explain them to you when you walked out on me at breakfast."

"I feel bad about that. Let me finish my story about Leon. The Seven is the reason I'm here."

"Sorry. Go ahead."

"When word got up to the newsroom that Leon had been killed, there was the usual commotion. A couple of metro reporters and a photographer headed for the street. Leon was a good editor, but as I told you earlier, not very friendly. He was kind of off-putting. He wasn't really close to anyone in the newsroom, although he sometimes talked to me and asked my advice about stories. He thought I was a good reporter. Anyway, I was sitting at my desk lost in thoughts about Leon being dead and what I had told you earlier about overhearing the words 'the seven' in a phone call he made last week when a part-time news clerk, who's a student at American University, came to my cubicle almost in hysterics. She was crying and carrying a Post envelope with my name on it. She said between sobs that earlier in the afternoon Leon had given it to her with instructions to give it to me if anything should happen to him. He swore her to secrecy. Tears streaming down her face, she handed me the envelope and walked away."

Jake spoke for the first time since they had entered the hotel room.

"What was in it?"

Max reached into his jacket pocket and pulled out a piece of Post letterhead. He handed it to Jake. On it were five handwritten words: "The Seven must be stopped!"

＊

Jake took the stationery from Max and studied it.

"Have you shown this to anybody else?"

"No. I didn't know what to do, so I called Bill."

Bill stood up.

"Max, your reaction to what I told you at breakfast this morning was my fault. I should have approached you more directly and honestly. But I think I can fix that."

Bill turned and opened a closet where the safe was located. After punching in the combination, he pulled out the two manila envelopes. Using the postmark as a guide, he opened the second one he had sent to Max from Santa Fe.

He handed Max the copies of the pictures, making sure that the copies of the back of each picture were matched with the correct photo.

Max seemed confused.

"I don't understand what I'm looking at."

Bill went over each picture with Max, explaining the importance of the dates on the backs.

"Max, these pictures were left for me to find by Warren Holden. You knew him. You know what a smart, straight-shooter he was. These pictures are the real deal. They show that NASA and the government have been lying about UFOs and about the face on Mars. Now settle back and listen. I'm going to tell you what happened to me a year ago when I went out to Indiana to help a friend."

"Is this the guy whose daughter you said was abducted by a UFO and later killed by The Seven."

"Yes, but don't walk out on me this time."

"I think I need a drink first."

"Scotch okay?"

"Sure."

Bill walked over to a small desk, picked up the phone, and punched the number for room service. Within fifteen minutes they had a fifth of single-malt Glenlivet, a silver container of ice, and three crystal glasses.

Jake opened the bottle and poured a round. They had said little waiting for the Scotch. Max had studied the pictures over and over again.

"Are you ready?"

"As I'll ever be."

Bill started at the very beginning, telling Max about the mysterious phone call he had gotten from Paul in Indiana. He recounted all that had happened last year in Jefferson and almost all that had happened since. He described his relationship with Morgen and laid out in detail their nighttime ride to meet Colonel West. He told Max about the file West used to force his silence; his conversations with Warren Holden and Walter Jansen; the letter from West; and his meeting with Jake McCoy and their road trip for the mailings. He left out that he spent the night with Betty Holden. He also didn't mention Larry Sullivan, although he was aware that Max knew he was a confidential source.

An hour and a half and several drinks later, Bill paused.

"That's an outline of what happened and what we know. Now let me show you a couple more things."

From the envelope, Bill pulled out of copy of Colonel West's letter.

"You need to read this, Max."

Max read the letter very slowly and deliberately. When he was finished, he looked up at Bill and Jake.

"This is unfucking believable. I can see why you were afraid I might rush out and write a story if you told me everything. But not now. I don't want to end up like Leon Jenkins."

"There's more."

With that Bill handed Max copies of the lists and summaries.

"As I said, the lists I found in Warren's attic. He had left them there for me. The summaries we found in a secret compartment he built into a doghouse."

Again, Max read them slowly and deliberately. Every fourth or fifth name he would utter "Holy Shit" or "Jesus H. Christ."

"Jim Winston at the White House is a part of this murderous outfit! I've known him for years. We used to work together at The Plain Dealer in Cleveland. And the Senate majority leader and the CIA director. My God!"

Max poured himself another drink.

"These mailings of yours explain why things got so quiet a few days ago. Before then there was a buzz in the air. Not now. I can't fucking believe this. I mean, I do fucking believe it. What the hell are you ... we going to do?"

"Max, I promised you could have the story. And you can. You just have to hold off until the time is right. Until we figure out what to do. Will you help us? You know more about this town than anybody I know. We need you. Leon Jenkins was right: The Seven must be stopped. We just have to figure out how to do it before they make their big move. I think the mailings stalled them for a time, but not a long time."

"Count me in."

"Great. It's late. Let's get together tomorrow. I'll call you both in the morning and we can decide where and when. By the way, Max, Jake is staying at the Mayflower."

"Spook Central?"

Jake smiled.

Bill fell into bed exhausted and slightly drunk. He went to sleep immediately.

Bill was alone on a deserted beach. The sky was overcast and threatening. Huge waves thundered onto the shore in front of him. He looked around for Morgen but saw no one. He had never felt so alone. He sat down in the sand and put his head on his knees. Suddenly, the roar of the waves ceased, as though someone had muted the sound on a television. Bill looked up. Everything looked the same. The waves were crashing, but soundlessly. It was if he had suddenly gone deaf. Then he heard Morgen's voice. It seemed to come from all directions. She was calling his name. Then a phone began to ring. Bill fumbled for his cell but couldn't find it. Morgen called his name again. The phone rang again ....

Bill jerked awake. He looked at his watch. Three-twenty.

He picked up the bedside phone.

"Hello."

"Bill?"

"Yes."

"It's Max."

"What is it Max?"

"It's Jim Winston. He committed suicide a little before midnight."

The next two days were chaotic as Washington absorbed the news that the President's press secretary, a well-liked former reporter from Ohio who was popular with the media crowd, had killed himself. A bachelor, Winston lived alone in a third-floor apartment a few blocks from the White House. According to news reports, he slit his wrists with a box-cutter while sitting in his bathtub with the water running. A resident on the second floor in the apartment directly below Winston's noticed reddish water running down the walls of his bedroom. He called the superintendent. When there was no answer at Winston's apartment, the superintendent called the police. They found Winston dead in a bathtub of bloody water. People who knew him were dumbfounded. No one knew of anything in his life, work, or background that would have explained suicide. He left no suicide note. He had been the press secretary to the President since the start of his first term; he was always upbeat and quick with a joke. He had been dating a lawyer in the Justice Department. They were often pictured together at dinners and social events at the White House. The President, obviously grief-stricken, announced he would fly to Cleveland later in the week for the funeral.

Bill and Jake didn't see much of Max or each other in the days immediately following Jim Winston's death. In the case of Max, a glance at the front page of the Post explained why. Max was all over the story and would be traveling with the President to Cleveland on Air Force One. Jake was using the hiatus to work his CIA sources.

Bill was beginning to be a little concerned that he hadn't heard from Larry Sullivan but remembered that Larry had said finding out something about The Seven could take a couple of days.

Later in the afternoon, Bill was reading the Times in his hotel room when his cell phone alerted him to a text: "It would be great to see you again."

An hour later, he met Larry at their usual rendezvous point at the zoo.

Larry was not his usual, smiling self. Bill assumed it was because of Jim Winston's suicide, but Larry never mentioned it. Instead, he started off on a serious, lecturing note about The Seven.

"Jesus, Bill, you sure know how to pick 'em. Colonel West last year and now this Seven thing."

"What did you find out?"

"What I found out is that you need to drop this. I mean let it go. Get back to New York and write books. You're in way over your head. This is some serious top-secret shit, and it's being handled by the military. You must not get involved. You will screw up secret plans and operations that have been underway for months. Forget The Seven."

With that, Larry turned and walked away.

Later that night in the hotel, Bill tried to call Larry's cell. He got a recording saying that the number he had dialed was no longer a working number. He walked over to the window and looked down at the White House.

Is this what it's come to? After all the deaths, all the searching, and all the work? Has the bottom fallen out? Am I back where I started? Is Larry part of The Seven? If not, why did he change his number? Where does that leave me? And Jake? And Max? Three who know the truth but can do nothing except watch a disaster unfold?

— THE END —

THE FINAL BOOK OF THE TRILOGY

Book 3
SECRETS
coming Spring 2021

Bill Sanders and Morgen Remley are reunited and join forces in an effort to stop The Seven that takes them from New Mexico to the Oval Office.

ABOUT THE AUTHOR

Fred Ellis Brock is the author of the best-selling *Retire on Less Than You Think: The New York Times Guide to Planning Your Financial Future* (2nd Edition – Times Books/Henry Holt, 2008); *Health Care on Less Than You Think: The New York Times Guide to Getting Affordable Coverage* (Times Book/Henry Holt, 2006); and *Live Well on Less Than You Think: The New York Times Guide to Achieving Your Financial Freedom* (Times Books/Henry Holt, 2005). For more than a decade he was a business editor and columnist at The New York Times. For six years he wrote that paper's "Seniority" column and was the author of the "Off the Rack" media column prior to that. He has also worked as an editor and reporter for The Wall Street Journal, The Houston Chronicle and The Louisville Courier-Journal. He holds an M.Ed. from Temple University and a B.A. in English literature from Hanover College. He has taught undergraduate and graduate reporting and editing at New York University and Kansas State University, where he held the R.M. Seaton Professional Journalism Chair. He was a fellow at the Washington Journalism Center, with a concentration in public affairs reporting. He lives in Arizona, where he teaches at the University of Arizona and is a contributor to The New York Times and a featured speaker for the Times Journeys travel program. He is represented by the David Black Literary Agency and AEI Speakers Bureau.

Brock, while pursuing conventional journalism and teaching careers, has been interested in UFO sightings and science fiction since he was in high school. He is a member of the Mutual UFO Network (MUFON) and has witnessed unexplained sightings in the U.S. and Europe. He has interviewed scores of witnesses to UFO sightings for both articles and personal research; he has read widely on the subject. All this is reflected in the authenticity of *The Seven*.

9 781948 018920